The Twelve Step Pathway

The Twelve Step Pathway

A Heroic Journey of Recovery

Michael Cowl Gordon

ROWMAN & LITTLEFIELD
Lanham • Boulder • New York • London

Published by Rowman & Littlefield
An imprint of The Rowman & Littlefield Publishing Group, Inc.
4501 Forbes Boulevard, Suite 200, Lanham, Maryland 20706
www.rowman.com

86-90 Paul Street, London EC2A 4NE

British Library Cataloguing in Publication Information Available

Library of Congress Cataloging-in-Publication Data

Names: Gordon, Michael Cowl, author.
Title: The twelve stage pathway : a heroic journey of recovery / Michael Cowl Gordon.
Other titles: 12 stage pathway
Description: Lanham : Rowman & Littlefield, [2023] | Includes bibliographical references and index. | Summary: "Using the twelve step framework for understanding the inner work a person must do in order to overcome addiction, Michael Cowl Gordon walks readers through the journey to inner salvation and peace. Using the heroe's journey as the path on which to travel through these steps, he uncovers the deep work that it takes to be the hero in your own story"— Provided by publisher.
Identifiers: LCCN 2023016181 (print) | LCCN 2023016182 (ebook) | ISBN 9781538183267 (cloth) | ISBN 9781538183274 (epub)
Subjects: LCSH: Twelve-step programs. | Drug addicts—Rehabilitation. | Alcoholics—Rehabilitation.
Classification: LCC HV5801 .G66 2023 (print) | LCC HV5801 (ebook) | DDC 362.29—dc23/eng/20230509
LC record available at https://lccn.loc.gov/2023016181
LC ebook record available at https://lccn.loc.gov/2023016182

To my many patients, loved ones, mentors, and friends, both inside and outside twelve step programs, who have faced their life's challenges and demonstrated what it means to be heroic.

Contents

Acknowledgements

It would be impossible to mention by name all the people to whom I am grateful for their encouragement and support throughout the creation of this book. This includes a great many colleagues, mentors, and friends who have enhanced my life over the past many years. So I will name just a few key persons. First, my wonderful wife, Judy Gordon. Next, my exceptional daughter, Michelle Y. Gordon. I must thank my lifelong friend, Jack Kramer, who first read the draft of my manuscript and told me it needs to be published. I am indebted to the eight persons who wrote their stories for this book: Renee, Niall, Hawk, Steve, Youngblood, Susan, James, and Charles. Of course, these are not their real names. I must thank my agent, Don Fehr, who believed in the project, and Suzanne Staszak-Silva, my acquisitions editor at Rowman & Littlefield, who took a chance with an unknown author. There are many others whose help has been invaluable. I wish I had the space to name you all.

Disclaimer

Excerpts from AA materials are reprinted with permission of Alcoholics Anonymous World Services, Inc. ("AAWS"). Permission to reprint these excerpts does not mean that AAWS has reviewed or approved the contents of this publication, or that AA necessarily agrees with the views expressed herein. AA is a program of recovery from alcoholism only—use of the excerpts in connection with programs and activities which are patterned after AA, but which address other problems or in any other non-AA context, does not imply otherwise.

Introduction

Welcome to the world of heroic adventure and transformation. The message I hope to deliver is that everyone can be a hero. We are all challenged in life, most of us to a degree much greater than we had expected or hoped to be. Life is, indeed, difficult. There may be family conflict; physical or mental illness; financial struggles; work-related problems; legal difficulties; death of loved ones; and, for some, even more serious difficulties, including abuse, extreme poverty, homelessness, starvation, imprisonment, domestic violence, and war. Worse, in the midst of dealing with our struggle to survive in the world as we find it, often there is an even greater struggle going on: that of facing and overcoming ourselves. No, in the world in which we all now live, the hero is not called on to don a suit of armor, climb on a white horse, and slay an actual fire-breathing dragon. Rather, the dragon we are called to slay is the inner dragon, an aspect of the self that is remarkably elusive and self-destructive. The inner dragon may be so cunning that we are not even aware of its existence. Discovery and defeat of this dragon is the true objective of the heroic quest.

On my own journey, I have spent fifty years as a medical doctor specializing in the treatment of people with addictions. The experience of helping people identify and disable their own inner demons, if not slay them altogether, has been a great gift to me. In part, it has been a journey of discovering my own limitations. I cannot slay the dragon for anyone other than myself. Nor can I give anyone an exact map to negotiate the sharp curves and other obstacles they will encounter in life.

What I can do is encourage people to decide to take their own heroic journeys; to learn about who and what they are; and to make positive life decisions that will lead them ultimately to a place of healthful living, peace, and self-love. In my work, I have introduced patients to many resources that can assist them on this journey. The most potent of these resources has proven to be Alcoholics Anonymous.

The twelve steps of Alcoholics Anonymous have been instrumental in helping millions of people to reclaim their lives from various addictions and other difficulties that had previously defied resolution. The steps provide a blueprint that, if followed rigorously, will lead the traveler to the treasure, that of recovery, wholeness, and self-love. My first attendance at an AA meeting was as an invited guest. I was introduced to Wayne W., an AA member who had heard of my interest in working with alcoholics as patients. He quickly realized that I had a lot to learn about recovery. From the medical standpoint, I was well informed about the effects of alcohol on the liver and nervous system and the general health risks that were attendant to these patients. But at that time, medicine had little to offer to alcoholics in the way of achieving permanent abstinence.

Wayne brought me to a meeting held at the AA clubhouse on Carroll Street in Madison, Wisconsin, just off State Street, the main drag of the University of Wisconsin. It was November 17, 1972, a chilly Friday night. Even at that time of year, State Street was a party scene, loaded as it was with drinking establishments and thirsty students seeking release and merriment. The meetinghouse was full. There were probably around one hundred people in attendance, and what was striking was the jovial mood in the room. People were friendly, laughing, hugging, but at the same time serious about sobriety. After some preliminary readings and a prayer at the outset of the meeting, we were treated to the main event, three gentlemen who had come down from Green Bay to share their experiences with us. They each spoke for about fifteen minutes. I can assure you that their messages were powerful because, to this day, I remember something of what each of them said.

As I sat there, it occurred to me that there was a remarkable force at work in that room. Here were three alcoholic men from Green Bay sharing their recovery stories with around one hundred sober alcoholics in Madison right by State Street, where one wouldn't expect to encounter any sober alcoholics, especially on a Friday night. I thought that the odds of that happening by chance were close to zero. After the meeting, as people were socializing, I stood and looked at a wall hanging that listed the twelve steps. I decided to accept the proposition that the program worked because people were following the twelve steps and that, as they claimed, God was doing for them what they could not do for themselves. In that moment, I decided to dedicate my professional life to working with alcoholics where I could be useful and at the same time combine the power of spirituality (not religion) with my medical training. Now, a little more than fifty years later, I can say that it was the best professional decision I ever made, and I am immensely grateful to have been given the opportunity to have the career that I have had.

Another gift that I have been given is the ability to learn from my patients. A major step in my spiritual journey happened about twenty-five years ago, when I met with a new patient who was a cocaine addict seeking help. He told me that he was a follower of Joseph Campbell, and he asked me if I had ever heard of him. As it happened, I had heard of Joseph Campbell, but I was not well informed, so I asked him to tell me about his beliefs. He told me what I hear from a great many newcomers to recovery: He believes in a spiritual dimension to the universe, but he had no specific belief about God. He quoted Campbell as saying, "God is beyond all categories of human thought." That rang true for me, so I went home and obtained a copy of Campbell's *The Hero with a Thousand Faces*. I also read *The Power of Myth*, where I discovered the actual quote is "Eternity is beyond all categories of Human thought." Campbell goes on to say, "We want to think about God. God is a thought. God is a name. God is an idea. But its reference is to something that transcends all thinking."[1] So it is the same idea; we lack the capacity to think about God as God is.

I got the recordings of Campbell's conversations with Bill Moyers that were taped at George Lucas's Skywalker Ranch more than a decade earlier. I was very attracted to the heroic journey as a metaphor for life in general and for recovery in particular. I saw that the struggles my patients went through were indeed heroic in scope. Like many of my patients, sometimes I didn't know what to think about God. I had come to mistrust formulaic explanations of God offered by religions. One of the many things I had come to like about twelve step recovery was that it took no dogmatic position on God. That was left up to the individual who was walking the walk, so to speak. In the book *Alcoholics Anonymous*, it does say, "He was as much a fact as we were."[2] But it also says that what you believe is up to you, as long as you are *willing* to believe in a power greater than yourself.[3] (The program is based on the book, which is referred to in the program as the Big Book. It is from this book that the program acquired its name.) The book also states, "Deep down in every man, woman, and child, is the fundamental idea of God."[4]

Following Dr. Carl Jung, this suggests that the *idea* of God is an *archetype*, a fundamental sense or idea, carried along in the structure of the human personality in the collective unconscious. But the idea can manifest in different people differently. I believe that if people can understand recovery as a heroic journey, then it will give them a helpful perspective that will encourage them and increase their likelihood of success. In this book, I talk about the heroic journey based on the ideas of Joseph Campbell. I also review some key concepts of Dr. Jung, who interestingly had an inadvertent but crucial role in the genesis of AA. It is fair to say that it may well never have been founded without his influence on a patient who had been in his care.

In the last fifty or more years, many books have been written about the twelve steps, and others have been written about the heroic journey. However, almost nothing has been written that brings these two powerful forces together. With *The Twelve Step Pathway: A Heroic Journey of Recovery*, I combine the heroic journey and the twelve steps into an understanding of the immense powers of transformation that bring heroic travelers to living the life of their best selves, of spiritual awareness, and of repair of the world through service to others.

The book defines *addiction* and gives some scientific background to support the concept of addiction as an illness. I go through each of the twelve steps, showing what role each step plays on the heroic journey. I draw on the wisdom of many philosophers, theologians, poets, and psychologists as I take the reader on a journey through these pages. Some notable figures in addition to Bill Wilson, Joseph Campbell, and Carl Jung include Martin Buber, Paul Tillich, Howard Thurman, Carl Sandberg, Rabbi Abraham Joshua Heschel, Thich Nhat Hanh, and Dag Hammarskjöld. I also present throughout the manuscript stories of people in recovery. These were written in their own words. Storytelling is a powerful means of teaching. I hope these stories will help the reader to comprehend the relationship between the twelve steps and the heroic journey and to see how this concept can be applied to one's own life.

By understanding life as a heroic journey, people facing a seemingly insurmountable difficulty—whether it be addiction, physical or mental illness, consequences of traumatic life experience, loss of a cherished loved one, or having to come face-to-face with their own mortality—can have a life of success rather than failure. Indeed, we all are potentially heroic, and when engaged in the hero's quest, we add meaning to our lives and discover our true selves at depth.

I hope this book presents information, a way of looking at things, and a plan of action that can help people achieve their own heroic potential and live meaningful and gratifying lives. By reframing the alcoholic's life as a heroic journey and recovery as an adventure in that journey, people can begin to think about themselves less harshly. A person filled with self-hate who has already learned to numb feelings with drugs or alcohol will be compelled to continue with this self-medication and self-destruction unless presented with an alternative pathway. That pathway can be that of the heroic journey—and the twelve steps can serve as a GPS for that journey.

Most people would rather be a hero than a drunk. The idea of being heroic may develop slowly, but it will develop. Readers will benefit from the analysis of the stories of other people in recovery, people who may not be very different from themselves. At the end of the book, there is a workbook with numerous exercises to help readers think through their own situations. This is a book that can be reread many times. For example, a person working on the fourth step might want to consult that chapter to stimulate their thinking and understanding of how best to approach the step.

The book will be most effectively used in conjunction with other recovery literature, including *Alcoholic Anonymous*, *Twelve Steps and Twelve Traditions*, the recovery texts of Narcotics Anonymous and Al-Anon, and a great many others. I want every reader of this book to know that they have a journey to take and a story to tell. I wish everyone safe travels on the road to recovery. And now, let's begin with a story.

Jacob's Story

Wrestling with the Divine

The story we begin with on our journey through these pages is that of Jacob, the biblical patriarch. I tell his story because it is instructive and well-known. He did not start out in life as such an admirable character. He was something of a momma's boy and a manipulator. As Jacob set out on his own heroic journey, traveling with great haste to escape the murderous wrath of his brother Esau, from whom he had stolen his father's blessing, he stopped for the night, not at an inn, but on the open road, and sometime during the night, he had an extraordinary experience:

> Jacob left Beersheba and set out for Harran.
> When he reached a certain place, he stopped for the
> Night because the sun had set. Taking one of the stones there,
> He put it under his head and lay down to sleep.
> He had a dream in which he saw a stairway resting on the earth,
> With its top reaching to heaven, and the angels of God were
> Ascending and descending on it.
> There above it stood the Lord, and he said:
> "I am the Lord, the God of your father Abraham and the God of Isaac.
> I will give you and your descendants the land on which you are lying.
> Your descendants will be like the dust of the earth, and you will
> Spread out to the west and to the east, to the north and to the south.
> All peoples on earth will be blessed through you and your offspring.
> I am with you and will watch over you wherever you go,
> and I will bring you back to this land.
> I will not leave you until I have done what I promised you."[1]

Let's look at the backstory to put this event into context. According to the biblical text, God had promised Jacob's grandfather Abraham that he would make him the father of a great nation, and this promise was repeated to Jacob's father, Isaac. In the normal course of things, this promise would then extend to the eldest son of Isaac, Esau, born first, with his twin brother, Jacob, hanging on to his heel, trying to win this race. But no, let's look into the story further.

Jacob was born to Isaac and his wife Rebecca after Isaac prayed to God because Rebecca had been unable to conceive. Once pregnant, she carried twins, who were reported to have struggled with each other in her womb. The firstborn was Esau, and he was noted to be red and hairy, even at the time of his birth. Oddly enough, as the second twin emerged, he had a grasp on Esau's heel and thus was named Jacob. As they grew up, Esau was the favorite of Isaac, but Jacob was the favorite of his mother. Esau was a hunter, and Jacob pursued domestic tasks.

One day, Esau came home from hunting, and he was hungry. Jacob had a stew going on the fire, and Esau said, "Man, I'm so hungry I'm about to die. Give me some of that stew you have over there." Jacob offered a bowl of stew in exchange for Esau's birthright. It doesn't seem like a good deal for Esau, especially, if you think about it, he probably could have helped himself, and Jacob couldn't have done that much about it, Esau being big, red, hairy, and all. But apparently Esau lived in the moment, and in that moment, his birthright didn't mean that much to him. Or possibly, he figured when he needed to, he could have killed Jacob and taken it back. At any event, they struck the deal.

Later, Isaac asked Esau to go hunting for him and prepare a meal, following which, Isaac would give him his blessing. Isaac was elderly and seemed to think his days were numbered, so he knew he had better get on with the business of blessing his firstborn son, thereby conferring him with his inheritance in spirit and legally. Rebecca overheard their conversation and quickly cooked up a scheme with Jacob. She prepared a meal for Isaac, just the way he liked it, and got some lambswool for Jacob to cover his hands and arms, as Isaac had gone blind and would not be able to see which son came before him. She also gave him Esau's clothes to wear so that Isaac would think Esau had just returned from the hunt.

When the food was prepared, Jacob brought it to Isaac. Isaac's first words were, "Who is it?" Jacob lied and said he was Esau. Isaac was suspicious and questioned how he prepared the food so quickly. Jacob lied again. Then Isaac, still suspicious, wanted to touch his son to see which one it was. So Jacob approached him and let him touch his wooly arms and hands. Isaac was unconvinced and said, "The voice is the voice of Jacob, but the hands are the hands of Esau. Are you really my son Esau?"[2] Jacob lied again, so Isaac ate his meal, kissed Jacob, smelled his aromatic garments, and gave him his blessing. (My mother and I could never have pulled a fast one like that on my father. Isaac seems to be a willing dupe in this story.) Soon, Esau arrived to discover he had been tricked and deprived of his father's blessing. After some wailing and gnashing of teeth, Isaac gave Esau a blessing, too, but a poor substitute for Jacob's.

Esau was enraged and planned to kill Jacob as soon as Isaac died, which he anticipated would be very soon. (In fact, Isaac lived another eighty years.) Rebecca, once again eavesdropping or relying on her sources, realized that Esau wanted to kill Jacob. She thought it unwise to depend on Esau being patient enough to wait until the death of Isaac to kill Jacob, so she told him to go hide out with her brother Laban, who lived in a land far off to the east. Jacob made haste to leave, thinking that after a while, Esau would cool off, and he could return.

On the way, he stopped for the night, and had the incredible experience of the dream shared earlier in this chapter. Jacob woke up thinking that he had stumbled on the gateway to heaven, erected a monument, and named the place Bethel (Hebrew for *house of God*). As he did so, he offered a deal to God. Jacob promised God that if God kept his promise, then Jacob would let God be his God. Such a deal! Oh, and he offered God a tenth of his production.

The adventure continued. Jacob arrived in Harran, met his uncle Laban, and fell in love with his cousin Rachel. Laban told him that he could marry Rachel if he worked for him for seven years. Jacob agreed immediately, but on his wedding night, Laban switched daughters, substituting his older daughter Leah in the dark of the night, a cute reversal on the trick Jacob pulled on Isaac. Leah participated in the deception, possibly because she had no husband or prospects at that point (or as a woman had no choice). She was not as pretty as Rachel, described in the Bible as having "weak eyes," whatever that means.[3] Regardless, it was not a compliment, because it appears in the same verse in which Rachel is said to have a "lovely figure" and that she was "beautiful." Laban was unapologetic for the deception but let Jacob marry Rachel the following week in exchange for another seven years of labor. In the end, Jacob spent twenty years with his uncle and left for home with wives; concubines; children; and herds of goats, sheep, donkeys, and camels. He had become a wealthy man. His uncle was a shady character, but with God's help, Jacob got the best of him.

So Jacob achieved success in the far-off land to the East, and it was time to return home. While he didn't specifically refuse the call to return (an integral component of the heroic journey, described in the next chapter), he remained afraid of his brother and in that sense did not prefer to return home. In fact, he showed no interest in returning home until he feared that Laban would kill him for getting the best of him in their agreement on dividing the flocks of sheep and goats.

Once again, he left in a big hurry. On his way, he met more angels of God, although nothing else about this encounter is mentioned. Presumably, it would have been encouraging to Jacob. He sent messengers ahead to tell Esau he was on his way home and that he wanted to make amends, hoping to be received peacefully. The messengers returned with the news that Esau was coming to meet him with an army of four hundred men. Not good. Arriving back in Canaan, Jacob brought his entourage across the river and then crossed back to spend the night alone, presumably to be in prayer. Then he had an encounter with a man in another remarkable story:

So Jacob was left alone, and a man wrestled with him till daybreak.
When the man saw that he could not overpower him, he touched the
Socket of Jacob's hip, so that his hip was wrenched as he wrestled with
    the man.
Then the man said, "Let me go, for it is daybreak."
But Jacob replied, "I will not let you go unless you bless me."
The man asked him, "What is your name?"
"Jacob," he answered.
Then the man said, "Your name will no longer be Jacob, but Israel,
Because you have struggled with God and with humans and have overcome."
Jacob said, "Please tell me your name."
But he replied, "Why do you ask my name?"
Then he blessed him there.[4]

Wow, what an experience! There is a lot to unpack here, far more than I want to devote to it for our purposes. Jacob is in crisis in his life, at the threshold of his return home to face his brother, his life possibly near its end. The river symbolizes this threshold, the demarcation of the point where his old life transforms into the new. This is both a continuation, in a sense, of the adventure and a time to look inward, a look stimulated at least in part by his fear. His encounter with the man in one sense symbolizes this inner struggle with himself. However, the storyteller wants us to believe that it was a real physical wrestling match, making the point that Jacob sustained a significant injury to his hip during the fight. The name change from Jacob to Israel is a device often used in the Bible to signify a major change by God to the spiritual status of the person involved (Abram became Abraham; Sarai became Sarah). The following morning, Jacob, now Israel (although I continue to refer to him as Jacob, as does the narrator of the story), crosses the river, orchestrates an elaborate atonement ceremony, and makes peace with Esau.

Now that he has returned to his homeland safe, wealthy, and with his wives and children, we could be at the end of his story. We might say that, as we hear in fairy tales, that he lived happily ever after. But that is not what happens in real life, and in fact, he has a great many challenges and much pain and loss before he breathes his last. His favorite wife, Rachel, the love of his life, dies in childbirth; a son shames him by having sexual intercourse with one of his concubines; his daughter Dinah is raped; two of his sons wrongfully slaughter an entire community in retaliation for the rape; his favorite son, Joseph, fails to return from an errand and is presumed dead; and he has to leave his home again, this time for Egypt, because of a famine.

The message is clear. The heroic journey does not come to an end. Life is hard. And once the hero returns home successful in the quest, life is still hard. But the heroic journey will give the hero the capability of coping with life on life's terms. The boon Jacob has brought home is his progeny, the children who will found a great nation in fulfillment of God's promise. The boon he has acquired for himself is a spiritual awakening. It is of interest that what he has not gained is happiness; loss and grief weigh on him heavily for the rest of his life.

Chapter One

The Heroic Journey

A Quest for Redemption and Wholeness

This is a book about becoming heroic. A hero faces great danger, overcomes incalculable odds, and accomplishes what would have been thought (especially by oneself) impossible to achieve. Considering the fear and pain that such a person must experience in such an adventure, it is a role that few would desire. Yet more of us find ourselves in circumstances demanding heroism than one might imagine. In fact, I suspect that people who are never called on to be heroic are in the minority, if they exist at all. Some, of course, are heroic on a grander scale, such that their names and life accomplishments are household knowledge.

This is not a book for people who might want to become heroic someday. It is for people in the midst of a crisis, whose very lives are threatened and who must decide if they are going to face their situation, survive, rise above themselves, and then share their newfound knowledge with others in need of salvation. And it is for those already traveling such a journey who would like to gain a new understanding of themselves and of what their journey has been about and a deeper comprehension of why it is so important.

Classical mythology is full of stories about heroes. Well-known examples from the Greeks are Odysseus and Orpheus, from the Hebrew Bible are Moses and David, and from American history and folklore are George Washington and Davy Crockett. But there are lesser-known heroes and even more totally unknown or forgotten heroes but heroes nonetheless. Today, as I sit down to write, I am mindful of the passing yesterday of Hank Aaron, the legendary baseball player who grew up poor and Black in Mobile, Alabama; made his way to the Milwaukee Braves baseball team; and then to Atlanta when the Braves moved there in 1966, putting him back in the Deep South, where he had grown up oppressed by Jim Crow. He broke Babe Ruth's home-run record in Atlanta when he hit his 715th home run in 1974, amid multiple death threats and a torrent of hate mail. (He advised his Black teammates Ralph Garr and Dusty Baker not to sit next to him in the dugout if they didn't want to get shot.) After his playing career, he was a baseball executive and successful businessman. He was always a gentleman, never complaining or showing anger at the way he was abusively treated by people hanging on to their code of White supremacy.

Today's newspaper coverage was extensive, with many people quoted and using the word *hero* in reference to him. Hammering Hank Aaron did not have a goal of becoming a hero. His goal was to become a professional baseball player because he was good at it and because he hoped it would be his ticket to escape poverty. As Michael Murphy writes in *Golf in the Kingdom*, "Life is taking us on a mighty journey, if only we will go."[1] Hank Aaron did go, and my hope is that my readers will do the same. Taking the leap, we learn so much about ourselves and about life, and if we are fortunate enough to survive our adventures, we can, as Henry Aaron did, pass our experience and knowledge on to inspire others as they travel their own paths.

In this book, I use the heroic journey as a means of understanding, dealing with, and overcoming the difficulties encountered in life. The heroic journey is a type of myth. It is a story that includes several component stages: (1) the call to adventure; (2) the refusal of the call (or wish to refuse); (3) acceptance of the call and receipt of divine assistance or magical powers; (4) the adventure; (5) attainment of the quest; (6) the call to return; (7) refusal of the call to return (or wish to refuse); and (8) the return home with whatever boon or treasure has been acquired as the result of the successful quest. There are many variations. Sometimes heroes are killed, but they are always reborn in some form. It is easy to think in terms of life as a journey, and partly for this reason, we can relate our own lives to that of the hero.

Typically, heroes are minding their own business when they are presented with a challenge that appears on the face of it to be impossible to accomplish. For example, when God appeared to Moses in the burning bush, He instructed Moses to go to Pharaoh to demand that the Hebrew people be set free. Also typically, the first reaction of the hero is to refuse the challenge. The not-yet heroes have become comfortable in their lives, used to whatever their circumstances are, even though, to an onlooker or possibly even to themselves, they might appear to be miserable. In the case of Moses, he told God that he had a speech impediment that would make him ineffective in communicating with Pharaoh. Of course, God had an answer for this and for other objections.

Another element in the hero's tale is the assurance of divine or magical powers that will make it possible for the hero to succeed in a mission that is manifestly impossible to accomplish alone. Sometimes heroes refuse the call because they don't believe things can ever change or they will work it out on their own. God told Moses that He would be with him and help him. Indeed, God conversed with Moses frequently, told him what to say and what to do, and worked miracles that resulted in the Hebrew people being allowed to leave Egypt.

But the danger was not over, and soon Pharaoh gave chase, leading to more miracles, including the parting of the sea, the drowning of the Egyptians, and the provision of food and water in the wilderness. But Moses still had seemingly impossible odds against getting this horde of hundreds of thousands of people to the Promised Land. So, the return from the attainment of the objective, in his case, was immensely difficult, unmanageable by a mortal man. Finally, the Hebrew people were given permission to cross the Jordan River and assume possession of the Promised Land. Interestingly, Moses was not allowed to enter the Promised Land. He died just before the crossing. But the boon, as Joseph Campbell calls it, was delivered. In this story, the boon is threefold: the release from Egypt, the giving of the law at Mount Sinai, and the Promised Land.

Myth as a word is generally taken to refer to a story about something that didn't really happen. There is nothing to say that any given myth is necessarily wholly or partly untrue. From my standpoint, it makes no difference whether a story is historically true or not. What is important is the story itself and what it can mean to the hearer of the story. Probably the most important thing to understand about the hero's journey is that it is really two journeys: There is the adventure itself, and there is the inward journey as heroes discover their true nature and overcome their fears and shortcomings. This self-knowledge opens an entirely new realm of their lives, that of the spiritual, and the adventure is life changing. The journey is unique to each individual. There is no one right way to live life. All people must find their own truth.

In trying to understand this better, especially the inwardness aspect of the journey, we turn to Carl Jung and Joseph Campbell. This part of our own journey through these pages will lead us somewhat into the weeds, as we try to grasp what, for many, will be unfamiliar and difficult concepts. Part of the difficulty is the use of terms we may be unfamiliar with or that are used in a way that is new to us.

Dr. Jung's theoretical work had to do with the structure of the human personality. We needn't examine his entire structure, but there are a few points that are important for our purposes. First is his argument that the human personality does have a structure. This structure is determined, in part, by heredity. He says that there are certain aspects of human thought and experience that we all have in common and that are genetically determined. If he had known about the genetic code carried on DNA, he would have said that is the means of transmission. Most of the personality structure is at a level at which the person is not consciously aware. It is generally understood by the average person that there is a level of our existence that is at an unconscious level. We see evidence of this in dreams. We also have an awareness that we often do, say, or think things that seem to come out of nowhere. We may establish a goal and then sabotage it without understanding why. There is an unconscious aspect to a person's personality, the existence of which is not that hard to intuit, even if it is not well understood.

Jung says that the *structure* of the personality is hereditary. He uses the term *collective unconscious* to describe an aspect of this structure that carries ideas, images, and information known to our ancestors. Here we get more into the weeds. He says that this information is carried in the form of *archetypes*. An archetype, he says, is a fundamental idea or sense of something, and it elicits deep feeling. Mother is an archetype. The first encounter of the infant with the mother stirs something inside the infant that it recognizes as protective, nurturing, loving. Infant is also an archetype that elicits a deep desire on the part of the mother to nurture, love, and protect. Physical touching is pleasurable and reinforces these thoughts and feelings. Archetypes are carried by lower forms of life, as well. Newly hatched chickens, for example, will run for cover if they see the shadow of a chicken hawk cross their path. But the shadow of a pigeon, duck, or goose elicits no such response.

Campbell also talks about archetypes. He sees the hero as an archetype. Likewise, the monster that appears in heroic tales is an archetype. We see the monster archetype in the Bible with the Leviathan tamed by God as He brought order out of chaos; with Pharaoh, who enslaved the Hebrew people; and with Goliath, who was slain by the hero archetype David. We experience the monster archetype in our fears of the dark, the bogeyman, and Count Dracula. These monsters all represent the destroyer, that force over which we are helpless to protect ourselves. Thus, we have the need for the hero archetype for protection. Think of Darth Vader and Luke Skywalker as destroyer and hero archetypes.

Obviously, the collective unconscious will never be demonstrated by an X-ray or a laboratory test, so we can't say it has objective reality. But as a concept, it has great merit, and I would like to proceed in this discussion as though it carries a lot of weight. Most people would agree with it to some degree, even if they don't think in these terms. I would suggest, for example, that the *idea* of God is an archetype. People are born with such an archetype, and then the course of their lives determines just what this comes to mean to them personally. In *Alcoholics Anonymous*, it states, "Deep down in every man, woman, and child is the fundamental idea of God."[2] Clearly, according to this line of reasoning, the *idea* of God is an archetype.

The structure of the personality as described by Dr. Jung includes the persona, the ego, the shadow (the dark side), and the self. The persona is what we want others to see of us. We all to some degree put on an act to present a favorable impression of ourselves to others (and to ourselves). We may want to present ourselves as nice, pleasant, kind, and caring, or we may want to appear to be tough, formidable, decisive, and not to be messed with. The persona is well within our realm of consciousness. We are aware of the persona.

Next, we consider the ego. This term is used in different ways and in different contexts. My simplest understanding of ego in Jung's terminology is that it is *who we think we are*. It is the center of our awareness of ourselves. What it is *not* is the center of our entire personality. It is what is on or close to the surface. Looking at a landscape, we would be mistaken if we think that we see all there is to the landscape in seeing grass, trees, a pond, or whatever else. Beneath the ground, there is an entire world of activity: topsoil, worms, insects, minerals, rock, aquifers, molten rock, and the earth's core. In any given situation it may not matter if we don't think about what lies underneath the surface, but in some circumstances, it could be extremely important. People are like this. There is the surface, of which we are aware: in our present terminology, the persona, and the ego. And there is the universe of ourselves beneath the surface. From our standpoint, the most important thing to understand about what lies beneath the surface is that *it is largely immune to the control of the ego.*

Using alcoholics as an example, let's say that they have become aware that control of drinking has been lost. Let's say that they are now aware that it is a problem in their life and that control must be regained. To an alcoholic's amazement and chagrin, the attempts of the ego to take charge and achieve control are ineffective. Promises, oaths, resolutions, and efforts to regain control or stop drinking end in failure. There are forces beneath the surface that are more powerful than the ego to overcome. Unless alcoholics solicit aid, the attempt to confront themselves in their entirety will be unsuccessful. They will continue to be at odds with themselves and not understand why or know what to do about it. The components of the personality in this example lack coherence and integration. Both Carl Jung and Joseph Campbell, along with a great many other writers, talk about unity as a goal in life. Jung talks about individuation, the process whereby a person integrates the components of the personality to achieve a comprehensive whole. Wholeness is a major theme of the myths of which Campbell writes. In a way, it gets at a great challenge in life, that of returning to the creator.

An important aspect of the Garden of Eden story has to do with rationalizing the presence of evil in the world. Here, the shadow comes into consideration. For our purposes here, we must acknowledge that everyone has a dark side. People can be selfish, rebellious, hateful, jealous, lazy—the list goes on and on. For Dr. Jung, this aspect of the individual is an integral component of the personality. Life challenges us to both acknowledge this and to overcome it. Indeed, we accomplish this, we resolve this duality, by traveling the heroic pathway in our lives. And as we travel this road, we encounter Dr. Jung's deepest level of our personalities, which he terms the self. It is here that we are connected with God or, if you would rather, with the spirit of the universe. For people who find themselves connected spiritually in this way for the first time in their lives, it is a profound awakening. Realization of staying connected and remaining unified with a higher power requires work and sacrifice; it is one of the lessons learned on the journey. The twelve steps provide not only guidance to engage in this heroic journey but also the means to continue the quest for the duration of one's lifetime.

The call to adventure for the addict is the challenge to recover. This call has certainly come many times previously in the course of the addictive trajectory. Many half-hearted and some full-bore efforts may have already been made. But one day, in dire circumstances, the addict thinks he or she just can't do this any longer and must either quit or live a miserable life until dying a miserable death. So the call has been made once again, and finally, it is not refused. The addict may or may not have tried certain things before, like a twelve step program, a religious approach, psychotherapy, a geographic cure, switching to nonalcoholic beer or wine, or dozens of other thus far fruitless efforts. Some people who have tried AA or another twelve step program before may not be willing to try this route again because it didn't work or they didn't like some aspect of the program. There could be many reasons for the program failing initially, but most significantly, the failure to follow through with an initial attempt at recovery illustrates the second stage of the heroic journey: the refusal of the call to adventure.

Of the many sorts of people I hope to reach with this book, one type is the people who think a twelve step program is not for them for whatever reason. I hope to make a convincing case that a twelve step program is a prime example of a heroic journey, a way of thinking about recovery that may make it more appealing. Another person I want to reach is the one for whom twelve step recovery has been beneficial but who needs a fresh way of thinking about the process. I believe that the more different ways you can describe the same thing, the better you understand it. My hope is that many people who are either in recovery or are considering it will read this book and embrace the idea of being on a heroic journey. And if the book only helps a handful of people in salvaging their lives, then my effort will have been worth it. The rabbis say that a person who has saved a life is as one who saved the entire human race, because, according to the Bible, humanity started with one man. For at least some who need to move forward in their lives, I hope reading this book can stimulate the dawning of a new day.

Chapter Two

Bill Wilson and the Founding of Alcoholics Anonymous

Beyond His Wildest Dreams

Bill Wilson was born in 1895 in a small town in Vermont.[1] His parents divorced when he was quite young, at least in part due to his father's drinking. He saw very little of his father after the divorce and not that much of his mother either. His father was a granite-mining supervisor and moved out to western Canada. His mother moved to Boston to attend medical school. This left Bill in the care of his maternal grandparents, who did their best with him.

Bill suffered from insecurity, probably more than most teenagers, and always strove to prove himself. A turning point in his life came in his early teens when his grandfather, Fayette, casually remarked that only an Australian aborigine could fashion a boomerang. Taking that as a challenge, Bill spent that summer working on designing and making a boomerang. A big day in his life was the day he took his grandfather out to a field and demonstrated his boomerang, which he threw with such effect that its return almost took their heads off. Fayette was delighted and praised Bill to the skies, telling him that he was the number one man.[2] Bill was sent to boarding school, where he excelled in athletics, repeatedly having to overcome a sense of inadequacy by working at a skill until he had mastered it. This determination to solve a different problem in later life, his alcoholism, both served him well and nearly killed him, proving the adage that too much of any good thing can be a bad thing.

He drifted somewhat aimlessly after high school, but when the war came, he signed up and became an officer. It was in the military that he encountered alcohol. He seemed to do well as a leader of men.[3] After service, he married Lois Burnham, whose father was a doctor in New York City. He took night courses and gravitated toward Wall Street, where he worked different jobs and established some good connections. This was during the 1920s, a period of boom on Wall Street. Bill was one of the first people who questioned purchasing stock in a company that the buyer knew nothing about. He and Lois took off on a motorcycle trip around the eastern United States investigating companies. He found companies that were grossly undervalued, wrote up reports, and became successful.[4]

However, two circumstances interrupted his rise to wealth and fame. By the time he was in his late twenties, he had become seriously alcoholic. As time went on, he became more and more unreliable and impaired, damaging his reputation and employability. The other event that affected his success in the financial world was the stock market crash of 1929 that led to the ensuing Great Depression. Work was very hard to get, and the few jobs he did get, he lost because of his drinking.

By age thirty-four or thirty-five, he was unemployable, drinking all day, waking up with terrible jitters, and at times so depressed that he contemplated suicide. Throughout this period, he was determined to solve his drinking problem, applying the same determination that he had to the perfection of a boomerang. He managed to quit at times for a few weeks but never was able to establish permanent sobriety. He was hospitalized at a private facility, Towns Hospital, to dry out on four different occasions.[5] His wife supported the family by working as a retail clerk because Bill was not able to work at all for the last five years of his drinking.

In November 1934, an old drinking buddy of his from his younger days, Ebby T., called on him. Ebby had been able to quit drinking with the help of a Christian spiritual program known at that time as the Oxford Group, and he called on Bill to offer the program to him.[6] Bill, who was pretty much an agnostic, was moderately inebriated during the visit but not so much so that he did not remember what Ebby had said. A few days later, Bill decided to investigate the mission where Ebby was living. Arriving there drunk, he sat and listened to the testimony of men who had quit drinking, and he then answered the altar call, making a drunken spectacle of himself.[7]

But a seed had been planted and was on the verge of germination. A few days later, he took the subway back to Towns Hospital and requested admission for the fourth time. While there, he was alone in his room after receiving a dose of medication, and he called on God to show Himself if He was real. Bill immediately had a profound spiritual experience but feared he had lost his mind. Calling the doctor, William Silkworth, he told him what had occurred and asked if he was hallucinating. Dr. Silkworth told him he was sane and that, whatever he had experienced, he had better hang on to it. This was another turning point in Bill's life. A few days later, he went home and never drank again.

He was too weak for gainful employment, of which there was very little anyway. But Bill was thinking more about saving the world than of getting a job. In his typically grandiose way of thinking, he thought that if he could share what he had experienced with other alcoholics, then they, too, could quit drinking. He envisioned these newly sobered alcoholics sharing it with others until, by a chain reaction, thousands and millions could be saved. He spent the next five months talking to alcoholics in bars and hospitals, and the only drunk who was sober from all that effort was himself.[8]

He attended Oxford Group meetings and learned about their program. In the spring of 1935, he was working on a deal that would have gained him employment running a company in Akron, Ohio, and he traveled there for a board meeting. It did not go well, and the group he represented was voted down. Tempted to drink, he remembered that he always felt better after talking to another alcoholic. He called a local clergyman, who put him in touch with another Oxford Group member, and she in turn arranged for him to meet with Dr. Bob Smith the next day. Dr. Smith and his wife had been attending Oxford Group meetings for more than two years, but his drinking remained out of control.

When Bill met with Bob, he tried a new approach that had been suggested by Dr. Silkworth just a few days previously. Dr. Silkworth told him he had to start by talking to the new man about the disease concept of alcoholism, the "physical allergy combined with the mental obsession." Only afterward should he bring up the spiritual angle.[9] Bob Smith was the first person Bill took this approach with, and it worked. Bob had one more drinking episode a few weeks later and then never drank again. His sobriety date is taken as June 10, 1935, which is also given as the date of the founding of Alcoholics Anonymous.[10] (Members of Alcoholics Anonymous are typically referred to by their first name and last initial: for example, Bill W. However, there are two exceptions, the cofounders of AA, Bill Wilson and Dr. Bob Smith. Their surnames are so well known that it is pointless to try to protect their anonymity, and they are generally referred to as Bill Wilson and Dr. Bob Smith or Dr. Bob, as in this book.)

Bill lived with the Smiths for three months and then returned to New York. Both men devoted themselves to working with alcoholics, and gradually, groups formed in both cities. After two years, they had gathered about forty men and one or two women who were sober. They had no specific method but relied more or less on the Oxford Group approach to spiritual life. Bill was encouraged on the one hand that what they were doing was working, but on the other, he was frustrated at the slow pace of progress. He was also in dire financial straits. He was working full-time with alcoholics, and he brought in no income. In 1939, the bank foreclosed on their house.[11] For the next two years, he and Lois were homeless, living here and there through the goodwill of others.

One issue that Bill struggled with for years was depression. He went through energetic highs, where he was a whirlwind of productive activity, and other times, he was so depressed that he couldn't get out of bed. A seminal moment in his life occurred during one of these gloomy times. It was a dark and stormy night in December 1940. Bill and Lois were living in a tiny apartment above a clubhouse that some AAs had established. Sleet pounded above his head on the tin roof. Sometime after 10:00 p.m., Tom, the custodian, called to Bill from the bottom of the stairs.

"There's a bum from St. Louis here to see you," he said. Bill shuddered. He didn't want to see anybody, but he never said no when another alcoholic needed help.

"Oh, no, not another one. Well, bring him up," Bill called back.

Soon up the stairs came a man wearing a shabby raincoat. His dilapidated hat was crusted with ice. He leaned heavily on a cane. When he collapsed into the chair, Bill, who was still lying in the bed, could see that his guest wore a clerical collar. Thus Bill met Father Ed Dowling, a Jesuit priest from St. Louis. Father Ed had encountered a copy of the Big Book, and he saw many parallels between the AA program and the spiritual handbook of his order, the Spiritual Exercises of St. Ignatius. Bill knew nothing of these exercises or of St. Ignatius and had only heard of the Jesuits.

He and Father Ed took to each other, and in the priest, Bill discovered a man to whom he could talk about anything. As they spoke, Bill unburdened himself of things he carried within himself and had never shared with anyone. He hadn't found the right person to talk with until that night.[12] It was then that Bill made what was in reality a fifth step, and from that time onward, Father Ed was Bill's spiritual advisor; in effect, his sponsor. (Bill always said that Ebby T. was his sponsor because it was Ebby who had, in effect, brought the inspiration to him that set him on the path of recovery. As a practical matter, Ebby did not have the stability of recovery that would have qualified him to give good spiritual and program direction to anyone on a consistent basis.)

By 1937, the groundwork had been laid for the AA fellowship. Realizing this, Bill and Dr. Bob called a meeting of a group of around forty men in recovery, and after acknowledging that what they were doing was working, they planned their next steps to spread the message of recovery. Until this time, they were in what they called their "flying blind" period, proceeding on some experience and instinct but no formal program. Several proposals were made and discussed at the meeting, and ultimately, they agreed to proceed along three paths simultaneously: First, they would establish a chain of specialty hospitals across the country. Second, they would train addiction counselors to staff these hospitals. And third, they would write a book describing their method of recovery.[13]

The first two proposals, especially the hospital chain, would require money and lots of it. For the next year, Bill spent all his time trying to raise money. Because of his connections and power of persuasion (and that of his colleague Hank P.), he gained access to the richest people in New York, including the Rockefellers. The men heard from these tycoons that what they had was marvelous, and they wished them well, but they felt money would spoil it. They rubbed elbows with more than $1 billion but ultimately came away with less than $10,000, most of which was used to support the living expenses of Bill and Dr. Bob.[14]

Dr. Smith's medical practice didn't quite support him, especially because he spent almost all his time working with alcoholics, work for which he never accepted money. In the absence of hospitals, they saw no use for trained counselors. The work done out in the communities with alcoholics was all being done by the recovering members, work for which no fee was charged. If anything, new prospects were helped financially to a limited extent until they could get on their feet. This left only the third proposal: writing a book.

Hank P. had rented an office in Newark, New Jersey, from which he was running a small business selling auto polish and related supplies to car dealers and service stations. It was largely in this office that the Big Book was written. Ruth Hock was the secretary for the business, but mostly what she did was type as Bill dictated chapters and stood behind her.[15] While this sounds like a strange arrangement, it is even stranger because it was said of Bill that he would never stand if he could sit, and he would never sit if he could lie down.

Bill produced material and then brought it to meetings of the recovering group, where his writing was discussed. Sometimes, the discussions became heated. One topic of strenuous disagreement revolved around the concept of God. About half the membership was agnostic, and they believed that pushing the God angle too forcefully would turn away a great many people before they ever looked further into the program. This was eventually resolved with a compromise of inserting the phrase *as we understood Him* after the word *God*.[16]

The other debate had to do with the tone of the book. Bill was taking a "do what we say" approach in his writing. He even went so far as to write at a certain point in his manuscript that if the reader was unwilling to follow directions, then he might as well throw the book away. It was close to the last minute before the book went to press that he conceded and changed his *directions* to *suggested steps* for recovery.[17]

In a little over four years, Bill Wilson had gone from being a hopeless alcoholic whose wife had been advised that she would have to put him in an asylum within a year to a man who had become convinced that not only did he have a successful method for staying sober but also his method was reproduceable and others could take advantage of it as well. His dream of millions of sober alcoholics was the driving force behind his efforts to raise money, to write a book and get it published, and to develop contacts with influential people who could help with publicity once the book was distributed. In April 1939, the book was published, and its title was *Alcoholics Anonymous*. Like just about everything else in the book, the title was hotly debated.

It was from the title of the book that the society took its name.[18] Prior to that they were One Hundred Nameless Drunks, the Alcoholic Squad of the Oxford Group, or just nameless. Within the AA program, the book is simply referred to as the Big Book. By 1939, the groups in both Ohio and New York had broken away from the Oxford Group for several good reasons. They had different missions, the Oxford Group was Christian, and AA needed to be unaffiliated.[19] Despite the publication of the book, Bill faced monumental challenges in 1939. He and Lois lost their home, the promised publicity from *Reader's Digest* fell through,[20] and Hank P. relapsed.[21] Bill and Lois were beyond broke. Nevertheless, they did start to get some publicity. Books were sent out to people who started their own groups in cities around the country (e.g., St. Louis, where a Big Book found its way to Father Ed).

One of Bill's great concerns was that, once they got national publicity, they would be overwhelmed with requests for books and information, and they would be unable to handle the deluge. In 1941, an article by Jack Alexander in the *Saturday Evening Post* triggered the tidal wave, and mail poured in.[22] Somehow, Bill and his mostly volunteer staff managed to answer every request for information. More groups formed, and AA was on its way.

It is at this point in the story that what Bill accomplished was truly heroic. There had been temperance organizations in the past that had been successful for a time, but none had survived. Most remarkable was the Washingtonian Society, which formed in 1840 and had an astonishing growth to more than 500,000 members. Ten years later, it had fallen apart completely.[23] By comparison, four years after Bill Wilson and Dr. Bob Smith started their project, they were a group of about one hundred people. Once major growth began, though, there was a substantial risk of things getting out of control. As remarkable an accomplishment as starting Alcoholics Anonymous was, an even greater challenge was to keep it from destroying itself.

Bill understood what he was up against, and he managed it with the determination and skill that he had proven to have as a youngster mastering the crafting of a boomerang. While he had many wise people to consult with and advise him, he demonstrated an instinctive understanding of how AA needed to be organized and structured for long-term survival. At times, he pushed his ideas too hard and engendered resistance and resentment, but in the end, he was able to establish AA according to what ultimately has been proven to work.

Much of what was finalized was learned by trial and error. For example, the question of who can be an AA member was decided after a questionnaire was sent out to groups asking about their membership rules. After reviewing the responses, it was obvious that if all the rules were enforced by all the groups, there would be no membership at all.[24] So, the ultimate requirement for membership was anyone who had a desire to stop drinking. Based on this requirement, a person wouldn't even really have to be an alcoholic. But it works.

In 1950, two things of importance to AA happened. First, at a convention in St. Louis attended by thousands of recovering alcoholics, AA adopted the twelve traditions.[25] These are the guidelines that Bill worked on to keep AA on a sound footing as an organization. The other thing that happened was Dr. Bob Smith died. Dr. Bob's death underscored Bill's point that AA can't depend on the personality of one or two people.

For the next twenty-one years until Bill's death in 1971, he continued to write, speak, and provide leadership to AA, knowing that, after his death, the program would live on. Fifty years since his death, it is evident that he did well. Aldous Huxley said of Bill Wilson that he was the greatest social architect of the twentieth century, and *Time* magazine named Bill Wilson one of the one hundred most influential people of the twentieth century.[26] While this may be the case, it could never have been Bill's ambition. It demonstrates where one's journey can take one if a life is established on spiritual principles, doing the next right thing, one day at a time.

Chapter Three

Addiction

A Powerful and Baffling Disease

Not only are there many definitions of *addiction*, but there are also many terms used to describe the condition. Every few years, the medical profession changes the terminology. We have had *alcoholism*, *drug addiction*, *chemical dependency*, *substance abuse*, *substance dependency*, and others. The current terminology determined by the American Psychiatric Association is *alcohol use disorder*, *cocaine use disorder*, and so on.

In their diagnostic manual, *Diagnostic and Statistical Manual of Mental Disorders, Fifth Edition Text Revision* (*DSM—5-TR*), criteria are listed for each of the disorders listed under the heading of "Substance-Related and Addictive Disorders."[1] There is a reasonable likelihood that, in a few years, when *DSM—6 appears*, the terminology will have changed again. It is not a matter of political correctness. As more research is done, our understanding of both physical and mental disorders improves, so doctors can gain better understanding of what their patient's trouble is, as well as how best to treat the condition.

There is always an awkwardness when writing about this topic because of terminology. In this book, the terms *alcoholic*, *alcoholism*, *addict*, and *drug addict* are used when it seems most appropriate to do so. Also, not all addiction is substance related. Gambling, for example, can be very addictive. In fact, anything that can produce euphoria, a pleasurable high sensation, can be addictive. If the term *addict* is used in this book, it is as a generic term that applies to anyone who is addicted to anything, alcohol included. The same applies to the term *addiction*.

The American Society of Addiction Medicine (ASAM) defines *addiction* in this way:

> Addiction is a treatable, chronic medical disease involving complex interactions among brain circuits, genetics, the environment, and an individual's life experiences. People with addiction use substances or engage in behaviors that become compulsive and often continue despite harmful consequences. Prevention efforts and treatment approaches for addiction are generally as successful as those for any other chronic diseases.[2]

Here is a definition of my own that I have been using for years:

> Addiction is a chronic, progressive disease in which the afflicted individual has lost control over his/her use of a substance or a behavior, which causes a pleasurable sensation. As the result of this loss of control, this individual has developed significant problems in one or more areas of life, including physical health, mental health, and spiritual or social well-being. Early in the course of the illness and sometimes throughout the lifetime of the addict, they are not aware that they have this disease, a process referred to as denial.

The disease is characterized by tolerance, meaning increased frequency or amounts of use of the substance or behavior are required to produce the desired effect. For most addictions, there is a withdrawal phenomenon, in which the discontinuation of the substance or behavior leads to physical symptoms, such as perspiration; tremulousness; nausea; sleeplessness; and/or mental or emotional symptoms, such as restlessness, irritability, craving, anxiety, and depression. The withdrawal phenomena vary greatly from one category of substance to another and from one patient to another.

(Notice that I use the word *patient*. This term comes from the medical model in which I am trained. Social workers call their patients clients. Sometimes people with diseases are referred to as victims of their condition. I don't want to get tied up in knots over terminology, so for my own sake of comfort and convenience, addicts are referred to as patients when I talk about them in the context of diagnosis and treatment.)

The terms *disease*, *sickness*, *malady*, and *disorder* are more or less interchangeable. They refer to conditions in which physical symptoms (e.g., pain, loss of appetite, nausea) or mental or emotional symptoms (e.g., anxiety, depression, or distressing or compulsive thoughts and behaviors) exist, often along with impairment of function. It is worthwhile spending a moment on this because there are people who deny that addiction is a disease.

This may be because addiction has the appearance of being self-inflicted and not the result of a natural dysfunction or process, like cancer or diabetes. Others may have an intellectual or philosophical argument that addiction is not a disease. Still others have grown up in alcoholic homes, where they have suffered because a parent's or other family member's addiction affected them severely. Some such people may believe that saying addiction is a disease can give them an out and say it wasn't their fault that they acted that way. I have no interest here to debate any of these ideas, but at the end of the day, for me and for most of the rest of the world, addiction is a disease.

The term *chronic* in talking of disease means that the disease is incurable. Once it has developed, the patient must live with it. Actually, most noninfectious diseases (and some infectious diseases) are chronic. Even though treatments are available that may be curative (e.g., successfully removing a cancer before it has had a chance to spread), that is usually not the case. Even in the cancer example, the doctor can't usually say with absolute certainty that a cure has been accomplished. Spread may have occurred that may take months or years to manifest. Chronic diseases can be treated, often with great success, but relapses may occur. This is certainly true of addictions, but it is also often true of many other kinds of illnesses, such as migraine and gout. Patients with chronic diseases may be on a regimen to control symptoms or prevent progression. Such a regimen may include special diet, medication, exercise, or highly specialized treatments like kidney dialysis.

The term *progressive* suggests that, over time, the symptoms may become more severe, occur more frequently, or lead to greater dysfunction. Not all chronic diseases are progressive, but addiction usually is. An interesting and distressing phenomenon in the progression of alcoholism is that some alcoholics who abstain for years and then relapse are much worse than when they quit drinking previously. It is as though whatever abnormality of the mind and body that made such a person susceptible to loss of control continued to progress in the absence of exposure to alcohol.

I want to focus on loss of control as the element that defines this disease. There are two types of loss of control. The first is that, once having ingested an addictive substance or engaged in an addictive behavior, the person is generally unable to stop when it would be reasonable to do so. After stopping for a beer at a local club, an alcoholic may well spend several hours having one drink after another. Gamblers who stop for cigarettes at their local convenience store, where they just happen to have video poker machines, may decide to play for twenty minutes and not stop until all their money is gone. And once having initiated this process, it continues irresistibly into the next day and the next day and the next.

The other type of loss of control results from a mental obsession or craving that is triggered by the drink, bet, or whatever the person is addicted to. As noted earlier, Dr. William Silkworth treated Bill Wilson at Towns Hospital in New York City. Dr. Silkworth had extensive experience treating alcoholics, and he observed that the disease had two components, which he described as a "physical allergy combined with a mental obsession."[3] As far as allergy is concerned, he used that term descriptively and did not mean to suggest that there was a pathophysiologic allergic reaction. His point was that, if an average person takes a drink, they may or may not want another but in any event will reach a point at which they will stop because they want to stop. They know that another drink will have some sort of consequence, such as drowsiness, dizziness, or dysphoria, that they don't want to experience. Or they may have plans for later in the day or the next day that they are committed to and that could be disrupted by continuing to drink. The main thing to note, though, is that they just don't *want* any more. Drinking *decreases* their desire for more alcohol at a certain reasonable point.

However, for alcoholics, it is an entirely different story. Once alcoholics have taken a drink, they have an *increased* desire for alcohol. They desire the second drink more than they wanted the first one. The idea of allergy is commonly understood and therefore is useful in explaining this phenomenon. Most people who eat strawberries do so at no risk of adverse consequences. Others will break out in hives, or their lips will swell. The difference has to do with a physical/chemical difference in the reactivity of the body to strawberries. Dr. Silkworth's point was that the difference between people who are alcoholic and those who are not has to do with a physical/chemical difference in the brain's response to the administration of alcohol. He was right about this, even though the science of demonstrating the differences had not been developed. As a matter of fact, although a great deal has been discovered about the abnormalities in the brains of addicted persons, much remains to be learned.

Obsession is a powerful force in the mind. In milder forms, it can manifest as determined motivation, but in its full-blown appearance, it is a destructive force that can lead to disaster. As a patient once said to me years ago about Nancy Reagan's naïve "Just say no" campaign, "I said no, but the drugs said yes." It is the experience of the addict that the obsessive thoughts about drinking will ultimately lead to giving in to the drink, drug, or behavior, despite all their past experiences of disastrous consequences. So addiction is indeed a disease of both the body and the mind. And as I explain in later chapters, it is a disease of the spirit, as well.

The phenomena of tolerance and withdrawal explain from a standpoint of brain chemistry how people may become addicted to substances. A drug will have no effect at all unless it can affect a bodily process that is already going on or has the potential to do so. Brain function involves billions of nerve cells, each of which performs a function by communicating with other nerve cells. A nerve cell can have either one of two possible effects on the cell with which it connects. It can either stimulate it, or it can inhibit it—turn it on or off. These effects are executed by chemicals released at the nerve endings. The nerve connections are called synapses, and the chemicals are called neurotransmitter substances.

When a potentially addictive substance is ingested, one effect of the drug is to cause a release of dopamine in the brain region, known as the nucleus accumbens. Dopamine is a neurotransmitter. The nucleus accumbens is part of a group of structures in the brain referred to as the mesolimbic pathway. This pathway is stimulated in response to certain activities or experiences that need to be reinforced for people to maintain good health and to propagate our species. Thus, stimulation of this pathway, leading to the release of dopamine and the experience of pleasure, happens through eating, sex, exercise, playing games, conversing with friends, listening to music, or other enjoyable activities. The brain is designed to remain in balance. So if the mesolimbic pathway is stimulated by an external source, like alcohol, a compensatory balancing response occurs. The term for the balance achieved, not only in the brain, but also in any living system, is homeostasis.

If such stimulation is occasional and not potent, then the compensation is of little consequence. Whatever depressant effect is experienced as the result of drinking, such as relaxation, will be followed by a slight overactivity of the nervous system once the alcohol has been metabolized. Normally, this effect will not be noticeable. However, if the use of alcohol becomes habitual and as the amount of alcohol increases, the rebound overactivity can become noticeable in the form of morning jitteriness, anxiety, or rebound insomnia. It is this phenomenon of rebound overactivity of the mesolimbic system and connected structures that leads to physical dependency. The individual comes to need the substance (alcohol in this case) to feel well enough to function. In the case of alcohol, the withdrawal effect can become extreme, leading to epileptic seizures and delirium. Indeed, alcohol withdrawal can be fatal. This is an example of how physical dependency and psychological dependency can occur simultaneously.

It is a wicked trap, and once people reach this stage of dependency, they seem to be unable, if stopped, to resume their use of alcohol or other potentially addictive substance or behavior without slipping right back into this vicious cycle. Once this neurological pathway has been established, the brain has no way of correcting the maladjustment. So once an abstinent alcoholic resumes the use of alcohol, this pathway is reactivated. One drink will call for another and another as the addiction is reactivated, and often it becomes worse than it had been previously.

It has also been observed that use of a drug in a different pharmaceutical class can trigger relapse. For example, an alcoholic who decides to use marijuana after a period of alcohol abstinence is at great risk of resuming drinking. The reason for this is that, at some point, the mesolimbic dopamine response is not drug specific. It is a system designed to stimulate the experience of pleasure, a sense of euphoria. Once stimulated in this manner, the craving for the drug of choice can easily be triggered.

For example, I recall treating a young man for alcoholism after he got a second citation for driving under the influence of alcohol (DUI). He agreed that he needed to maintain permanent abstinence from alcohol and planned to do so. However, he also planned to resume his use of marijuana, and I was unable to convince him otherwise. Two weeks after he left treatment, he got his third DUI, having already relapsed on alcohol. Marijuana had stimulated his mesolimbic pathway, triggering craving for his drug of choice, alcohol. Other examples abound, including gambling addicts returning to gambling after having a few drinks.

Another pattern we often see is people switching addictions: for example, from one class of drugs to another. Many heroin addicts I saw after their service in Vietnam had quit using heroin upon their return to the States, but they became severely alcoholic. Compulsive overeaters often become alcoholic after weight-loss surgery has prevented overeating.

Denial is another phenomenon that is always present to some degree, sometimes profoundly so, in addiction. Denial is a psychological defense mechanism designed to protect the ego from experiencing painful reality about itself. Ego defense mechanisms are part of the normal personality structure, and everybody has them. They are innate and operate at the unconscious level. Denial is a process in which an individual is blinded to a reality in plain sight to others (unless they are also in denial).

Along with denial goes rationalization, another ego defense mechanism. In the case of denial, the person simply doesn't see what others see. In the case of rationalization, what is now visible is explained away with such excuses as "I've been under a lot of stress," "I drink because I like the taste," "I can quit any time I want to," "I never drink and drive," "I drink no more than anyone else who I hang out with," and "If I ever [fill in the blank] I'll quit." The excuses offered are endless and rarely are overcome by rational argument. Addicted people must hit bottom to finally face the reality of what they have become, of what has happened in their lives.

Denial and rationalization are frequently used by the family and friends, as well. There are entire textbooks devoted to the scientific understanding of addictions. Judith Grisel's *Never Enough: The Neuroscience and Experience of Addiction* is excellent, and there are many others. Readers who are interested are encouraged to do further study on their own.

Renee's Story

Amazed by the Gifts

The gifts of the program of Alcoholics Anonymous never cease to amaze. Even the seemingly bad occurrences encountered in my sober life have always turned out with a silver lining. One of my greatest fears in getting sober was that life would get boring—the party was over. Little did I know that the encouraging words my counselor offered once I landed in a treatment center: A "wonderful life awaits me" if I can commit to a sober life. Nothing could have been more true.

Being the fourth of six children, with a large gap between myself and the older three, I was exposed to the drug culture of the sixties at an early age. My first experience was smoking marijuana at the age of eleven. I didn't know what it was, but after putting up a fuss about going out on the family boat for the last spin of the season with my older sister, she offered me a joint. A few days later, in 1971, I entered sixth grade in the parochial school I attended. New to the curriculum was drug education. We were taught that marijuana use led to heroin use, and fear of impending doom took over. A few months later, I was diagnosed with rheumatic fever and was certain that I was being punished by God for having gotten high on drugs.

At that time, I was one of the brightest students, president of my class, and a competitive swimmer. Up to that point, I had never failed at anything, but at the end of that school year, I was disqualified in a swim meet (for an inadvertent and inconsequential rule violation) that cost my relay team a gold medal in the Junior Olympics. The humiliation was overwhelming, and when I got home, my sister once again offered me a joint. I know today that it was my first conscious decision of using something to take away the uncomfortable feeling. And it worked!

My first drink was on a Sunday afternoon that same year, when my parents offered me a Manhattan. Interestingly enough, neither of my parents were alcoholic—a cocktail on Sunday when my grandmother would come for dinner and other celebratory occasions were the only times alcohol was served. The night before this, my older sister came home extremely intoxicated, and I believe my parents thought they would rather give me a drink than have me experiment with friends. The taste was nasty, but I remember the warm and giddy feeling and then proceeded to the kitchen to find a few more ounces left in the mixer. No one was watching, so I downed what was left.

That memory came back to me twenty years later after reading "The Doctor's Opinion," which was one of my first assignments after arriving at the treatment center.[1] Understanding the craving alcohol produced once ingested and the insatiable desire for more was crucial to my breaking the denial about being a true alcoholic. My marijuana use became a daily habit from my early teens. Alcohol was harder to come by, but whenever the opportunity presented itself, I would drink to excess. For whatever reason, I had a tremendous capacity to consume more alcohol than whomever I was drinking with and rarely got sloppy or had the awful hangovers I saw others experience.

I watched my parents go through some painful times with the behavior of my older brother and sister and assigned myself to being the good girl, which required a lot of sneaky behavior. To my detriment, I managed to get away with engaging in activities that were inappropriate for a young teenager.

Whenever I question if there is a God who had my back despite my behavior, I bring up the memory of sneaking into New York City one night at age fourteen to attend a concert, dropping acid, and missing my train home. I slept in a park that night until I could get the first morning train home, hitchhiked from the station, and showed up all perky from having "slept at a friend's house."

After graduating from high school with high honors and falling in love with one of my teachers, I went away to college and nearly flunked out my first year. Drinking became an almost daily activity, and the hangovers were starting to kick in. I made the decision to return to my parents' home and enrolled in the local college to be close to my boyfriend.

In addition to attending classes, I was working in a restaurant at night and learned the wonders of doing cocaine. I could drink greater quantities of alcohol, stay up all night, and make those morning classes. My grades improved, but once I thought I had it mastered, I kept pushing the envelope, so by my third year, the grades were slipping again.

I wound up marrying that cute teacher at the end of my junior year, and quite to my dismay, the party was now over for him. He took the responsibility of being a husband seriously and left his teaching position for a corporate career, and we bought our first home. That wonderful man stuck with me as my alcoholism rapidly progressed over the next ten years. I continued to carry on, forgetting I was married at times and would stay out all night—thanks to the abundance of available cocaine—and return home after he had left for work. By now I was a daily drinker—always a few cocktails after my work shift, regardless of having to go to class in the morning—and nights off always included some sort of lubrication.

Now into my fifth year of college, with maybe three years of credit, I learned I was pregnant. My first pregnancy was one I was not ready for—I knew it meant I would have to stop drinking and doing drugs. My uncle was going to celebrate his ten years of sobriety, and I was asked if I would host a party for him. We were sure to get one of those big urns of coffee, which I somehow know went hand in hand with AA meetings. At the same time, I had a full bar stocked at one end of the kitchen for the "normal" guests. I poured myself a bourbon and ginger ale and wound up spitting it out. The taste was awful, and I thought I had accidently poured scotch. Same thing happened after very carefully making a second drink. I didn't drink the rest of the day and the next day got my seemingly bad surprise after taking a pregnancy test. By the grace of God, I did not drink through that pregnancy.

I was keeping a stash of money for a big celebration once my daughter was born—another memory that surfaced years later when learning about the obsession of the mind when it comes to alcohol. Something miraculous happened, and the obsession to drink was lifted. I was finally the responsible wife and mother to now two daughters and close to finishing my degree. By now we had moved into our second home.

My husband was traveling on business, and friends had what seemed like exciting careers, but I felt stuck with two very young children. That overwhelming feeling of wanting to escape began to set in, and I decided to get my hands on some cocaine to help me study, which led to having a few drinks to level off the high, and the vicious cycle started up again. The sneaky behavior shifted from hiding my drug abuse from my parents to hiding it from my husband.

All this while, I had the tremendous support of my parents and in-laws, who lived close by. There was so much to be grateful for; however, all I could focus on was that the fun was over. My husband was too serious about life. A big blow came when he was offered a transfer, a wonderful career move for him. I was unable at that time to look at this opportunity with excitement. The fear of moving away from my parents and taking away their only grandchildren, my perception of disappointing them, and the idea of leaving my partying friends and drug connections were overwhelming. During the months leading up to the move, my cocaine use escalated to a point where I was staying up for three or four nights in a row. My husband would be gone for weeks at a time, and that was a license to drink and drug—didn't I deserve it?

The surprising thing was my mother saying how happy she was for us and that it was time to cut the cord. At twenty-seven years of age, my thoughts and behavior were infantile. Shortly before the move, I confessed to my husband that I was using cocaine to excess, and I was scared. He assured me that I was rightfully under a lot of pressure in keeping everything together in his absence, and everything would be fine once we moved.

The next four years was when my drinking escalated. I was sneaking cocktails before he came home from work and encouraging him to go to bed while I got things ready for the next day, only to stay up until all hours of the evening drinking—many times drinking myself into oblivion. The cocaine was no longer an issue, as it was no longer readily available, and I thought I had outgrown smoking marijuana. However, I always kept it on hand and would get high on occasion.

After one really scary night of drinking, my husband confronted me, and I told him I thought I had a problem and agreed to go to an AA meeting. He accompanied me, and we were met with open arms. What didn't sit well with me was the word *God* scattered throughout the steps and traditions posted on the wall. I had stopped practicing my faith and felt hypocritical praying, knowing deep down I was living a life that was in so many ways immoral and outside the scope of the teachings of the religion I was raised in.

It was suggested that I commit to attending ninety meetings in the next ninety days and to get a sponsor. The gentleman that made these suggestions asked if I could be there the following night, and I agreed. Much to my relief, on the ride home, my husband came up with a game plan that he would come home early from the office twice a week and help out on weekends so I could get to a few meetings a week. I returned to the meeting, met the gentleman who invited me back, and asked if he would be my sponsor. Much to my disappointment, he told me it didn't work that way and introduced me to a woman who was available to be my temporary sponsor.

For the next forty-five days, I attended a few meetings a week and met with my sponsor on occasion. I had begun smoking pot daily once again. I was invited to her home one evening for a social gathering of her sober friends and learned that many of them had been heroin addicts. They expressed amazement that I was only a few weeks sober and had my act together. I perceived this as an indication that I really wasn't one of them.

I continued to compare myself to others in the meetings, as there were so many things I hadn't encountered—DUIs, needles, incarceration, and so on. On day 45, we hosted a dinner party, and much to my surprise, my husband asked me if I'd like to taste the wine he had uncorked for our guests. I clearly remember that moment, which was more than thirty years ago, as I was extremely surprised and didn't have the tools to decline the suggestion. I drank one glass of wine, and after the guests left, I offered to clean up and told him I'd be up to bed shortly. Needless to say, there was wine left over, and I proceeded to help myself. My drinking proceeded for another miserable three years.

During this time, I was convinced that I would come up with the magic recipe for being able to drink and stop at the appropriate time. Oftentimes I was successful and would manage to get to bed at a reasonable hour. Looking back on this, I can see the confusion this caused to my husband. As our book describes, "While the alcoholic who keeps away from drink, as he may do for months or years, he reacts much like other men."[2]

A frightful and clear illustration of this is a period of time when I was working toward a business designation and preparing for an exam. I left the house one evening to go to the library to study, and when I returned home, the car was gone, and my husband and daughters were not home. When they returned, my husband marched upstairs with both girls in his arms and put them to bed. I asked where they had been, and he told me that he was out looking for me in some of the bars I would frequent, sure that I was "due" for another spree. I had not been drinking and in my mind was practicing good behavior, so I naturally copped a resentment—how dare he think that? It was the justification I needed to start drinking again.

As our book describes, the progression of the disease was ever apparent. I picked up right where I left off. After arguing with my husband at home, I would go out at night and oftentimes not return until the next morning. I refused to go to AA, which my favorite bartender (and newfound source of cocaine) referred to as a program for losers. My husband had had enough, and we began talking about a divorce. He was offered another job transfer and gave me the option of staying where I was or returning to family. I angrily answered that I would move with him in order for the girls to be close to both of us.

Our plan to separate after the move was kept a secret from his employer and our families. We took advantage of the provisions of his company relocation benefits and purchased a home that I would live in with our daughters. In making the home selection, I remember surveying the appealing floor plan that would allow for ways to hide my drinking. The plan was for my husband to rent an apartment; however, when I arrived in our new southern location with a job opportunity waiting for me, my husband informed me that he had not signed the lease and he would like to stay in the house until the girls and I were settled. He would help in my transition to working full-time. Up to this time, I had always had flexible and part-time work engagements. He also made it clear that, if my drinking sprees continued, he would take custody of our daughters.

The exciting challenge of my new job, along with the geographic change and fear of the humiliation of losing custody, was enough to keep my drinking under control for a few months. My husband would travel on business, and I began taking those opportunities to drink while he was away. That restlessness and irritability would kick in upon his return, and eventually I fell back into my old pattern of going out, finding a local bar where I met a few others who drank like I did, and decided I'd be happier if we went through with the divorce. At least I'd have every other weekend to be able to go out and have fun. We started seeing a divorce counselor with sessions both private and together. My first assignment was to attend an AA meeting. My northern arrogance kicked in, and I refused to do so; these southerners just wouldn't get me.

Shortly before he was to move out of the house, I returned from work one evening, and my youngest daughter was not well with what we thought was a stomach virus. We took her to the emergency room, and she was immediately taken into surgery for an appendix rupture. When we were told that she would be hospitalized for the next ten days, we agreed that we would take turns staying with her each night. I argued with my husband for him to take that first shift—I desperately needed a drink. It was a few minutes past the time that alcohol could be purchased; however, I managed to convince a gas station/convenience store attendant to sell me a six-pack of beer. I was not a beer drinker and did not like the taste, but I needed that comfort that any alcohol would give me.

Thinking my life situation was finally at a place where I could be happy, I deservedly drank when the girls were away with their dad. That lasted a few months until the day I was caught. There were a few scary times when I was out drinking at night and driving home drunk. I started a relationship with someone I met in the local bar who could keep up with me. My job was ending, and I was fearful of having to have to look for a new one. Knowing that the time off could be dangerous in keeping my drinking under control, I'd made a commitment to stop on March 1.

The next seventeen days were spent obsessing over a BYO party that was advertised in the local pub. Because my niece was in town and was available to sit with the girls, I decided to attend. While purchasing a bottle of Jack Daniels to bring to the party, I decided at the register to go grab a second bottle so I could have a drink before I left. I was sloppy and totally intoxicated before leaving the house. Driving home that night, I was seeing double and remembered asking God to please get me home safely. As I pulled into my driveway, I scraped the side of my car on the garage, putting a big dent in the rented vehicle I was driving.

The hangover was intense the next morning, and I began a drinking spree. I received a call one afternoon from my ex-husband to check in, and he asked if I had been drinking. The next thing I remember is waking up in my bed. It was dark, and the girls were not in the house. I phoned their dad, and he told me the girls were with him, they would not be coming home, and I was done. There was an empty bottle of wine in the trash and a near-empty half-gallon of vodka on the counter.

I was caught and immediately called my father, who had recently suggested that if I ever wanted to visit the place my now-sober younger sister had just returned from, he would make the arrangements. When I asked for help, he immediately booked a flight and told me I'd be flying out to Pennsylvania in the morning. The family joke was this was a spa, but no, it was a treatment center that followed the teaching and suggestions of the twelve steps of AA.

For the first time in my drinking career, I had the shakes while checking in at the airport. There was a layover that was extended to ten hours, and I roamed the airport, a few times nearly entering a bar, but a powerful force kept me from stepping over the threshold. When I finally arrived in Pennsylvania, I was met by a driver. The bar was still open at the airport, and he asked if I'd like to grab a drink. My response was "No thank you, I'm done." That was not me speaking, and today I believe there was divine intervention at play.

Upon arrival, I was put into detox, which I argued was not necessary. When I awoke the next morning, I was given a complete physical and released to my room. That afternoon I met with a counselor, and she laid out the plan for my remaining stay. My first assignment was to read the "Doctor's Opinion," which absolutely broke my denial about my alcoholism. It sparked that memory of my first drink that my parents offered me twenty years earlier.

The remaining weeks in treatment were a gift I will be forever grateful for. All the same suggestions were made that I had heard years earlier at my first AA meeting, but the most crucial one for me was to begin looking for the similarities in others' stories and to stop comparing myself out. Every employee of the treatment center was in recovery, and I was surrounded by sober individuals from all walks of life. A big obstacle was the need for prayer—asking God to keep me sober. There was a very thick wall built up that left me feeling hypocritical in doing so.

For the first week, I was alone in the room, and the first night that a roommate was assigned, I was unable to sleep due to her snoring. I marched to the nursing station and demanded to be moved across the hall to an empty room. The nurse smiled, handed me earplugs, and suggested I get on my knees and say a prayer to help me sleep. Needless to say, I was not pleased, but left with no other choice, I did as she suggested.

It wondrously worked, and when I woke up the next morning, I started to let down my guard. Something eerie was happening; maybe these people knew what they were talking about. There were numerous written assignments, and in writing my first step and remembering all the dangerous situations I had put myself in, I was beginning to see that something, someone had my back. I was lucky to be alive.

In the middle of my stay, I woke up from a vivid dream. I was sitting on a couch with a former professor whom I was extremely fond of. She was holding my hand and said, "Renee, you can do so well when you want to." When I returned home, there was a letter from my father with a clipping of her obituary. Unbeknownst to me, she had been a nun at one time. This was one of the many occurrences that helped break down that wall of accepting the help from a higher power—whom today I call God.

During the exit meeting at the treatment center, the results of my physical were reviewed. The doctor dismissing me expressed concern that perhaps I had not hit my bottom. Despite the extreme amount of alcohol I had consumed during the last ten days of my drinking, I did not have any elevated liver activity. I was in good physical shape, and the odds of me staying sober were not in my favor.

That character defect of defiance had actually turned out to be a blessing. I was going to prove him wrong. I was full of fear in leaving the safety net of treatment; however, something was different. I had an underlying sense of hope for the future. One of the most useful tools was to pull up the memory of my last humiliating drunken time when the thought of a drink crossed my mind. That, coupled with saying the Serenity Prayer numerous times throughout the day, did wonders for me. The obsession to drink was lifted.

A requirement for leaving treatment was to have a temporary sponsor. Another wonder of this program was the ability to have made a connection from one thousand miles away with a woman who agreed to fill this role. Like me, she was a single parent with two daughters. I made the commitment to do ninety meetings in ninety days—and my days in treatment did not count. This woman suggested I think of *God* as the acronym for "good orderly direction" and ask for this when feeling doubtful or defiant; this was another step in breaking down that wall. She, too, promised that a wonderful life lay ahead should I choose to commit to the program.

For the first time in my life, at thirty-two years of age, I had to seek employment. All my previous jobs had been handed to me. After a few unsuccessful interviews, I received a call with a job offer I had not interviewed for. My sponsor suggested that I use this opportunity to give thanks to my higher power, as this was where the credit was due. I continue to do my best to acknowledge God whenever gifts are bestowed on me.

In navigating through my first few weeks, I took it upon myself to interpret *temporary sponsor* to mean that I had to find someone else to be my permanent sponsor. I attended a noon meeting near my workplace and met a woman whom I asked to be my sponsor. She agreed but cautioned that her job required extensive travel. She had a phone I could reach her on—not common for this era. The following day, she picked me up for a different noon meeting in her beautiful convertible sports car, and I thought I had really chosen the right woman. She had the material things I thought at the time to be of so much importance.

A few days later, my youngest daughter was diagnosed with a brain tumor. My girls were ages six and seven when I quit drinking. Thank God I was sober and able to cope with this dreadful situation at that time. Doing what I'd been taught so far, I called my sponsor, and she shared that her husband had recently been operated on for the same condition. We spoke everyday through my daughter's hospital stay. A vivid memory that I continue to hold onto is walking into the chapel at the hospital, getting down on my knees, and asking God to watch over my daughter. I believe it was my first conscious act of sincerely practicing the third step (and eleventh step) of our program. The thought of drinking did not cross my mind during this time, and I was barely four months sober. What a contrast to my behavior ten months prior, when she was hospitalized for her appendix.

The surgery was successful in removing the tumor; however, there was some residual paralysis. A close friend and former partying buddy came down to visit, and we took the girls to an outdoor Moody Blues concert. Halfway through, my daughter wanted to leave, and my self-righteousness kicked in. I was resentful. After putting the girls to bed, my friend pulled out a joint. Despite learning that, for me, a drug is a drug, I took a few hits. The next evening, we were out to dinner at a place I knew was a danger zone—they served the best of my favorite cocktail—and the compulsion to drink was back with a vengeance. I was miserable and knew deep down that I had broken my sobriety.

The next morning, I attended my home group meeting, and halfway through, I shared what I had done the night before, asking if I needed to pick up a chip to start over. The room was divided—some sharing that AA was about the desire to stop *drinking*. Many of the members at that time had not experienced the drug culture I was raised in. I stood up in tears and asked for a chip. It was time to start over, and the next right thing was to call the woman who had been my temporary sponsor and ask her to take me through the steps.

The fourth step was commonly mentioned in meetings as being the guarantee to maintaining sobriety. At the time, I could only list my fear of snakes and resentments toward a few individuals, so my sponsor suggested I keep a pad of paper by my bedside and ask God each night to help me with this step. After doing this for a few weeks, I miraculously woke up in the middle of the night, and a long list of fears and resentments came pouring out.

Another wonderful suggestion I heard was to schedule an appointment to do my fifth step. I know now that this was a crucial step in my continued sobriety. After spending many hours with my sponsor, she advised me to go back and read the first three steps in the *Twelve and Twelve*.[3] I did so in reverse order, and in reading the third step chapter, I had an overwhelming sense of knowing I had been working this step throughout. Most importantly, I knew that I no longer wanted to be the person that I had been.

The timing on completing this step could not have been better planned. My first year in sobriety proved to be a crash course in living life on life's terms. My older brother passed away from AIDS later that year, my ex-husband filed for an annulment so that he could remarry in the Catholic Church and then proceeded with the wedding prior to the granting of the annulment. That seemingly bad exercise, which I strongly resented, gave me a beautiful gift. His responses to the numerous questions he answered presented me as a caring and responsible mother when I wasn't under the influence of drugs and alcohol. The annulment was granted on the basis of emotional immaturity on the part of both parties. A huge amount of guilt was lifted.

The night of the wedding I attended a second meeting and upon arrival was asked to be the speaker. The room was filled with a busload of folks from a treatment center, and I was given the strength to honestly share my story. Walking out of the room that night, I was filled with that wonderous calm and gratitude that continues to embrace me at different times in my journey.

Now in my twenty-ninth year of sobriety, my biggest fear is losing this incredible gift. Staying close to the fellowship, surrounding myself with sober friends, and continuing to work with my sponsor has allowed me to remain on this path through the ups and downs. My father passed in my tenth year of sobriety, and standing at the cemetery a few days before Christmas, one thousand miles from my home down south, I felt an arm around me. It was a close buddy from my original home group. In my twelfth year of sobriety, I made a move across the country to marry the love of my life—a gentleman I had dated for eleven years. We had waited to tie the knot because we each had two daughters and were committed to doing what was best for them until they were of college age.

Making the move and leaving the security of my close-knit circle of sobriety required a return to the basics of the program. I did another ninety meetings in ninety days and oftentimes found myself slipping into moments of self-pity, despite now having what seemed to be everything I wanted in life. It was a challenging transition, and I'm forever grateful that we both used the tools the program offered us to get us through, sober. Six years later, he passed away from cancer—two weeks short of celebrating his twentieth anniversary in sobriety. The outpouring of love and support I received from our fellowship eased the grief and deep sorrow of losing my husband. The thought of a drink or a drug never crossed my mind.

A few weeks ago, I was driving to the airport, taking in a beautiful desert sunrise, to pick up a close friend. The song "You've Got a Friend" came on the radio. While I was in treatment, we would gather in a circle every evening, holding hands, and listen to this song. I was brought back to that memory, and it touched my heart strings in that wonderous way of being overcome with gratitude. The friend I was picking up was a woman I had met at one of my regular meetings that she was attending for the first time. She was about fifteen years sober at that time and shared at the meeting that she had just lost her husband the previous day. Approaching her after the meeting, I offered her my number. My seemingly bad experience led me to another of the countless meaningful friendships I've made in sobriety. The journey continues to be challenging at times, it never gets boring, and I'm forever grateful for the divine intervention that led me to our life-changing fellowship.

Chapter Four

The Call to Adventure

Steps 1, 2, and 3

STEP 1: "WE ADMITTED WE WERE POWERLESS OVER ALCOHOL—THAT OUR LIVES HAD BECOME UNMANAGEABLE."[1]

The anticipation of starting a journey is typically accompanied by a mixture of feelings. One generally feels some level of excitement at the thought of new and different experiences: going someplace new, starting college or a new job, taking a vacation, dating someone new, or going to visit old friends. Along with the excitement there can be a certain amount of concern, possibly even fear. In these examples, we may worry that the weather on our vacation will be bad, that we won't do well or like the new job or new school, or that the date will be unpleasant.

Other journeys could be on an adventure we dread. We may be on our way to meet with an oncologist who will tell us what the treatment plan is for our newly diagnosed cancer or that of our loved one. Possibly we are embarking on a legal dispute that could cost us our jobs, our money, or our freedom. Sometimes we are simply uncomfortable with the idea of change. Whatever our circumstances, we may have become comfortable with our situation and worry that a change will lead to an increased level of discomfort or loss of control.

Sometimes the call to adventure can be dramatic and glorious, such as Moses being called by God from the burning bush. When alcoholics receive the call to adventure, though, you'll seldom hear harps or singing angels. Alcoholics receive the call when waking up on the bathroom

floor in a pool of vomit; waking up in jail, once again, not remembering just how they got there; or waking up in bed with a stranger, who
is also in the dark about the events that led to this disgraced condition.
Or they receive the call when they are fired by the boss who gave them
one last chance. I had a friend who received the call to adventure when
he walked into his garage one morning to find the front end of his truck
caved in and covered with blood. How had that happened? The last
thing he remembered was being at a bar drinking with friends.

In AA terminology, it is called hitting bottom.[2] For gambling addicts,
it can be finally getting caught embezzling money from their employers,
losing the family home after gambling away all the family money, or not
being able to send a child to college because the college fund has been
emptied at the slots. One can just imagine the humiliation that a sex addict experiences when the call to adventure comes. But of course, without
such a feeling of despair, humiliation, or abject self-loathing, no amount
of self-honesty will be sufficient to occasion an admission of defeat.

I know of a man who had swindled another man out of his life sav-
ings. The victim of the crime had committed suicide, and the perpetrator
had ample opportunity to think about what he had done, sitting in jail
for nearly ten years. He admitted to himself that it was only because
of his uncontrolled drinking and, additionally in his case, drug use and
gambling, that he lived a life entirely inconsistent with his own values.
He remembered the many promises he had made to himself and to
others that he would get his behavior under control, promises that he
made with great sincerity. But he had been fighting a losing battle. Sitting in prison, he admitted to his innermost self that he was powerless
over alcohol, drugs, and gambling. He heard the call to adventure, the
challenge to change his ways. Once released, he joined AA; worked the
twelve steps; and never drank, drugged, or gambled again. In truth, he
had received the call many times but had refused it. Sitting in prison,
realizing his responsibility in the suicide of the man he had swindled,
he accepted the call at last.

In other cases, no great tragedy has occurred. Sometimes it is no
more than a sudden recognition of what had been in plain sight but not
seen. It might be having a close friend expressing deep concern over
the change in a person. It might be the disappointment on the face of a
child whose basketball game one had failed to attend because of stopping for a "quick one" after work and then closing the bar hours later. It

could be drinking too much at a party and embarrassing one's spouse. In every case, the receiving of the call requires the recognition that not only is something dreadfully wrong with one's life and that it has been for quite some time but also, at some level, he or she has been trying to or at least meaning to correct the situation and has failed utterly. There is the sudden recognition that one's best efforts have failed to prevent a state of demoralization and defeat. It is from this situation, and from no other, that change can occur.

Meister Eckhart writes, "Truly, it is in the darkness that one finds the light, so when we are in sorrow, then this light is nearest."[3] AA historian Ernest Kurtz quotes Bill Wilson, who related what he learned from William James's *The Varieties of Religious Experience*, in *Not-God: A History of Alcoholics Anonymous*, "But nearly all [spiritual experiences] had the great common denominators of pain, suffering, calamity. Complete hopelessness and deflation at depth were almost always required to make the recipient ready. The significance of all this burst upon me. *Deflation at depth*—yes, that was *it*."[4] Yes, that *is* it: deflation at depth. Until one can experience that sense of despair and helplessness, the call will not be either heard clearly or acted on.

It is the prideful ego that represents the obstacle to the admission of defeat. For just so long as people hold on to the notion that they are the architect of their own destinies; that they have total control over their thoughts, actions, and the outcome of their efforts; that they are, in effect, God, there is no hope of peace, happiness, or communion with others as a member of the human race. For years, alcoholics run on a self-generated power impulse fueled by alcohol, laboring under the delusion that they are in charge of themselves and the world around them. Until that delusion is destroyed, until the reality behind the self-aggrandizement is exposed in stark clarity, until the alcoholic admits to powerlessness, things will only get worse. In a state of near hopelessness, the addict confesses defeat, entirely uncertain if indeed there is another way.

Having made such an admission of defeat, helplessness, and powerlessness, where can one go next? Suicide will occur as an option, taken by some. In fact, few are the addicts who have not considered suicide. Fortunately, the idea is abhorrent to most for a variety of reasons, including religious prohibition, the finality of the act, not wanting to hurt loved ones, or not wanting to appear as taking the cowardly way out.

In a sense, the act of self-destruction can only be taken from a position of having retained the right to be God. It is the ultimate taking of control, of asserting absolute authority over oneself. It is ironic that the most definitive act of self-control is the act of self-destruction. I do not recommend it.

Alternatively, if one can somehow recognize that bottom has been reached, then the choices are to wallow in it or to address the problem by taking some new action. Indeed, defeat can be turned into victory, a fact that has been testified to by many. Chuck C., a widely respected speaker and writer in AA circles, says, "I think losing yourself in life guarantees finding yourself in God."[5] And here is Bill Wilson's first Christmas message to AA members: "Nor can men and women of AA ever forget that *only through suffering* did they find enough humility to enter the portals of that New World. How privileged are we to understand so well the divine paradox that strength rises from weakness, that humiliation goes before resurrection: that pain is not only the price but the very touchstone of spiritual rebirth."[6] Eckhart Tolle advises in the face of hopelessness, "Become an alchemist. Transmute base metal into gold, suffering into consciousness, disaster into enlightenment."[7]

In answering the call to adventure through the twelve steps, alcoholics need to be prepared to radically restructure their way of thinking about important aspects of themselves and their life. That the twelve-step program works is beyond question at this point, but under what conditions is it most likely to be effective in bringing about the necessary transformation in a person's life? Very few people have successfully recovered using a twelve step program in isolation from others in recovery. Success is much more likely to occur for those who involve themselves in a community of recovering people. In such a community, newcomers find people with whom they can readily identify as having suffered with the same deadly malady that brings them to the group. They can learn from what the already recovering members did and how they did it, what brought them out of their misery onto a new road to good health and freedom.

What is most remarkable to a newcomer walking into an AA meeting for the first time is the laughter heard in the room. These are people who seemingly have returned from the disaster that their lives had become into a joyful way of life, free from the self-loathing that they must have once experienced. And these people are welcoming and appear to be glad to see the newcomer, reaching out a hand in warm welcome, offering a cup of coffee, engaging the newcomer in conversation. And the people are disarmingly honest. They say they are alcoholics, they talk about their drinking experiences looking back and laughing at themselves, and they tell the newcomer that what they have found is available to anyone who wants it.

And so a glimmer of hope is seen, a faint flickering light at the end of a dark tunnel, a possibility of emerging from the darkness. Newcomers are offered a chair, and as the meeting begins, they wonder what comes next, what will they have to do to get from where they are to where these people appear to be. They look forward, finally, into a future of possible peace and release from their trap, where they can stop hating themselves and their lives and stop regretfully looking backward at their failures. In such an experience as this is hope born, and they have started the heroic journey of recovery.

STEP 2: "CAME TO BELIEVE THAT A POWER GREATER THAN OURSELVES COULD RESTORE US TO SANITY."[8]

Lack of power, that was our dilemma. We had to find a power by which we could live, and it had to be a *Power greater than ourselves.*[9]

Thus in the Big Book, we find a clue to the secret that had heretofore eluded people in their attempts to free themselves from the stranglehold of an addiction. They had thus far failed to succeed at controlling their lives because they *lacked the power to do so.* According to the experience of AA, to succeed they had to look outside themselves for the power to succeed. Maybe this was something that had gone against their independent, self-directed nature, or possibly it had never occurred to them to get outside help, or possibly they had sought outside help, even of a spiritual nature, but failed to overcome their difficulties.

There is a saying in AA that describes the initiation into the recovery process: "We came; we came to; we came to believe." Admitting defeat, we arrived at the doorstep of AA (we came). Stepping inside, we realized that our database was incomplete; there was more to drinking and quitting drinking than we realized (we came to). And seeing the success others were having, we believed we could have a new life, as well (we came to believe).

A life without hope is a dreadful ordeal. A life without purpose or meaning seems hardly worth living. Those who are preoccupied with self-loathing, obsessed with the perception of life's unfairness, mired in regrets about past actions, filled with self-pity, and who feel abandoned by the God they were taught about as children and in whom they once believed suffer terribly through each day of their lives. Such people are legion, out in society by the millions. Not all of them have addictions, of course. Happily, for those with other problems, as well as for those who are addicted, hope is available. What is required is a willingness to give up on the old narrative, the one that doesn't work and therefore must not be true.

An interesting question is, Why do people insist on clinging to the old narrative, the one that doesn't work? There must be many reasons, some of which I have already suggested: the belief that alcohol or drugs are not only not the problem but also are the only thing that provides the power to keep them going; the belief that as long as one's problems are someone else's fault, they have no need to look at their part in them; and the fear that an attempt at recovery will end in failure, further proving one's helplessness and incompetence in dealing with life. These are just examples, but it is a fact that seldom will someone seek help immediately when confronted with a new difficulty, and some will never seek assistance. It is important to understand that resistance is natural. In the concept of the heroic journey, I have named it the "refusal of the call."

At some point in the lives of most people with such misery, a door opens, and an opportunity presents itself to answer the call. At such times, an event may occur and not necessarily a dramatic or catastrophic one. It might just be a chance meeting with someone, the triggering of an old memory, a dream, a song heard on the radio. Whatever the trigger, just for a moment, one is open to admit that things are out of control and is willing to try to get some help. This is the "we came to" part of the experience. "We came to believe" can happen when one meets with someone, whether at an AA meeting or with a therapist, a friend, or an addiction professional, who tells them that there is hope and points them in the right direction. Hope is what they have been living without. And what does one have to come to believe? Simply that there is help available, that life can change for the better.

Step 2 may occur slowly. It doesn't have to happen all at once. All that is required is a beginning, a willingness to look at things differently and to adopt a new course of action. Gabriel Marcel writes, "Hope is for the soul what breathing is for the living organism. Where hope is lacking the soul dries up and withers."[10] The drinking alcoholic has been deprived of life-giving hope for a long time. The addict takes the second step when it is recognized that it is time for a change and when a decision is made to move forward on a new journey.

Just what kind of a "power greater than ourselves" are people supposed to believe in that can straighten out their thinking and their lives, that can restore them to sanity? This is where much of the resistance is found. (Very few people at any stage of addiction recovery will question that they either are or have been insane.) In Western culture, people talk about God as viewed from a Judeo-Christian point of view. If I mention God, most people will have a very good idea of what I am talking about (or think they do). When I talk about God in this book, the bell that will ring for many if not most readers is just that God: the Big Guy in the Sky.

However, there are many who will say they believe in *something* but are at a loss to go much further about exactly what they do believe. For some, a belief in nature, the universe, or some other nondeity suffices. Many simply say they do not know what to believe, and then there are those who are true atheists—they do not believe in God. What I want to make clear here is that I am not expressing my own viewpoint on this matter, other than to say that any God powerful enough to have created and sustained the world I live in is entirely beyond my comprehension. In the introduction, I wrote about Joseph Campbell and his assertion that we lack the capacity to think about God as God is. Milton Steinberg writes, "We cannot know God completely. At the essence of God—what He is in himself—we can only guess; and of His manifestations and works we comprehend only that shred which our senses can grasp and our mind can conceive."[11] Aldous Huxley quotes St. John of the Cross as having written, "One of the greatest favors bestowed on the soul transiently in this life is to enable it to see so distinctly and to feel so profoundly that it cannot comprehend God at all."[12] And Father Ed Dowling states in his simple, straightforward manner, "If you can name it, it is not God."[13]

At the same time, many people have specific creeds or beliefs that represent the absolute truth to them about God. Far be it for me, in my own ignorance of the subject, to challenge anyone's belief. I am saying that what is true for you is not necessarily true for the next person. There must be room in the world for individual points of view. I might even suggest that, while the God of my understanding does not change, people as individuals will hear the message differently. So if I talk about God in this book, and I do a lot, please make that mean for yourself whatever makes the most sense to you. And if I refer to God as "Him" from time to time, I am only trying to preserve coherent sentence structure; I do not view God as an adult male with a white beard. Ultimately, in my view, the collective unconscious carries a sense of numinosity, a spiritual awareness of the divine that connects one deeply with the experience of loving and being loved by a higher power.

Again, what are people to do when they are at the start of this heroic quest and they are not sure about God or what to believe about God or to whom God has been represented as vengeful or dangerous? In *Alcoholics Anonymous*, the author makes a useful suggestion: "We needed to ask ourselves but one short question. 'Do I now believe, or am I even *willing* [emphasis mine] to believe, that there is a Power greater than myself?' As soon as a man can say that he does believe, or is *willing to believe* [emphasis mine], we emphatically assure him that he is on his way."[14]

So the only requirement is to be *willing* to believe in the existence of a power that lies outside of oneself. Frankly, this is a low bar to jump over. Such a power could be something as simple as the power of the group. It is obvious that a group has power that is greater than the sum of its individuals. However, I must admit that I have heard suggestions to try believing in a tree or a lampshade. A lampshade can keep the glare out of my eyes, but it will never keep me or anyone else sober. I have also heard people suggest believing in a doorknob, another ridiculous idea, until you think about the metaphor of opening a door into a new world.

Once a person has agreed to consider that there is a power greater than himself or herself, things can change for the better. This is the step away from despair and toward hope. And how different does that feel! At the beginning of the journey, we are not living with pure hope, nor are we perfectly free, but we have made a start. We have the glimmer of a vision or a hope, if you think about it, of what might be possible as we progress on our way to possess things beyond our imagination.

To take such a step requires courage. Peter J. Gomes in his introduction to Paul Tillich's *The Courage to Be*, says,

It takes a great deal of courage and imagination to believe that God is on your side when you are suffering or losing. To believe in love in the face of hatred, life in the face of death, day in the dark of night, good in the face of evil—to some, all of these may seem hopelessly naïve, wishful thinking . . . but, to Tillich, all of these are manifestations of enormous courage, the courage of confidence in more than the sovereignty of fact and appearance.[15]

Having come to believe that a power greater than ourselves can restore us to sanity or having expressed a willingness to believe, it is time for the next step in the journey. Be prepared, for it is a big one.

STEP 3: "MADE A DECISION TO TURN OUR WILL AND OUR LIVES OVER TO THE CARE OF GOD AS WE UNDERSTOOD HIM."[16]

Thus far on the heroic journey, our heroes have heard the call and overcome their resistance to answering it. They have recognized the hopelessness of continuing to live in the same manner that they have been living. Furthermore, they have come to believe that there might be another way, heretofore unrecognized, that may make life bearable or even rewarding and enjoyable. Having arrived at this point, it is now time for our heroes to get into action. The action is not the turning over of one's will and life to a higher power. It is *making a decision* to do so.

There is a formidable obstacle that must be overcome in deciding to give up one's will: the hyperinflated ego. The ego has a great need to stay in charge, to keep the wolves, real or imagined, at bay. To overcome this grandiose ego, a great (can we say heroic?) act of courage is required—and at a time of great distress and anxiety. At such a time, the temptation is to hold on even harder to one's old coping mechanisms. That this temptation is resisted and overcome reflects the profound degree of desperation at which the alcoholic has arrived. Nothing but a supreme act of courage will do to make the necessary decision to turn things over to God entirely, holding nothing back. It is a decision to embark on an adventure, having little idea of where one is going, what will transpire, or when one will arrive at the destination. André Gide has said, "One does not discover new lands without consenting to lose sight of the shore for a very long time."[17] And from Mickey Hart, drummer for the Grateful Dead, we hear, "Adventures don't begin until you get into the forest. That first step is an act of faith."[18] Indeed, courage and faith are essential components on the heroic journey.

There is a three-word phrase in this step that may escape notice or, if noticed, may seem superfluous. A friend attended an AA meeting while out of town. He knew nobody at the meeting, and no one knew him. The topic was the third step, and my friend offered a thought about the step during the discussion. After the meeting, an older gentleman walked up to him, tilted his head to one side, and said, "The step says to *the care of* God," and he walked off without waiting for a reply.

My friend was beyond annoyed, and as he drove to his hotel, he thought about the interaction. He had not been given an opportunity to respond. His ego was bruised because he had thought of himself as already possessing great wisdom about the step. But in truth, he had never noticed that in fact it does say "to *the care of* God as we understood Him." Why? Bill Wilson was a good writer who chose his words with precision. What was the point of saying "to *the care of* God" instead of just saying "to God"? I don't know that Bill ever was asked this question. It occurs to me, though, that stating the decision as one of turning the will and life over to *the care of* God implies that, if this decision is made, God will *care for* one's will and life. This addresses the great distrust people have in others, including or possibly especially God, in delivering to them what they want and need. The third step requires a surrender of one's will. This feels risky and would never be undertaken unless a person has become convinced that continued reliance on his own self-will will inevitably lead to further disaster.

Surrender is an act that makes great sense in the face of defeat. That it is accompanied by a loss of face or a sense of humiliation is beyond question. But it has been the experience of countless people that, once that step is taken, it is followed by a feeling of relief that may not have been felt for years, if ever. It is the act that opens the door to a new life. William James writes, "Self-surrender has been and always must be regarded as the vital turning-point of the religious life."[19]

Dr. Harry Tiebout was a psychiatrist who took an interest in the AA program early in the 1940s. He was one of those doctors who was adept at learning from his patients. He might have been the first psychiatrist ever to refer his patients to AA. One such patient came into his office one day bursting with excitement. He told the story at the AA convention in 1955:

One Monday morning she entered my office, her eyes ablaze, and at once commenced talking. "I know what happened to me! I heard it in church yesterday. I *surrendered*!" With that word "surrender" she handed me my first real awareness of what happens during the period of hitting bottom. . . . It became ever more apparent that in everyone's psyche there existed an unconquerable ego which bitterly opposed any thought of defeat. Until that ego was somehow reduced or rendered ineffective no likelihood of surrender could be anticipated.[20]

Chuck C. says in *A New Pair of Glasses*, "Surrender is the thing that opens the door that allows us to get the help; because God, himself, cannot help us until we will allow it. The recognition of the need for help and the turning of our will and our lives over to the care of God and clearing away of the wreckage of the past is the beginning of victory."[21] Notice that he also uses the phrase "*the care of* God."

Bill Wilson, an agnostic until he had his spiritual experience, extensively addressed the alcoholic who was still agnostic or atheist and for whom the idea of surrender to a higher power was nonsensical, offensive, or both. He talks about this in *The Language of the Heart* (excerpted from the July 1960 book *AA Today*):

I had struck an impasse with which thousands of incoming AAs have since collided. Mine was exactly the kind of deep-seated block we so often see today in new people who say they are atheistic or agnostic. Their will to disbelieve is so powerful that apparently, they prefer a date with the undertaker to an open-minded and experimental quest for God. Happily for me and for most of my kind who have since come along in AA, the constructive forces brought to bear in our Fellowship have nearly always overcome this colossal obstinacy. Beaten into complete defeat by alcohol, confronted by the living proof of release, and surrounded by those who can speak to us from the heart, we have finally surrendered. And then, paradoxically, we have found ourselves in a new dimension, the real world of spirit and faith. Enough willingness, enough open-mindedness—and there it is![22]

Ernest Kurtz talked about Dr. Tiebout and what he learned about what is necessary for an alcoholic's recovery: "Dr. [Harry M.] Tiebout . . . recognized four elements . . . as playing an essential role in the AA program: 'hitting bottom, surrender, ego reduction, and maintenance of humility.' . . . He [Tiebout] wrote 'The specific part of the personality which must surrender is the inflated ego . . . the carry-over of infantile traits into adult life . . . a feeling of omnipotence.'"[23] Repeatedly, the importance of ego-reduction at depth is emphasized as a necessary condition of recovery.

Dr. Tiebout's reference to the feeling of omnipotence calls to mind the wonderfully famous phrase of Dr. Freud: "His majesty, the baby."[24] No human could be more self-centered and self-preoccupied than the infant. The infant has needs that demand immediate satisfaction. If it is hungry, it demands nourishment. If it is cold, it demands warmth. If it is wet, it demands a dry diaper. Humans must progress from this state of demanding self-preoccupation to a place where they can become patient, caring toward others, reasonable in their expectations, responsible to themselves and to others—in a word, mature. The failure to achieve these goals can be likened to the retention of the infantile ego. It is this ego that must be deflated for any progress in recovery or indeed for any true happiness to be achieved.

And there is nothing new about these ideas. Almost two thousand years ago, St. Augustine said that the supreme human task is that of surrender to God. He went through his own struggles along these lines, and once he was clear about the necessity for him to surrender to God's will, he delayed, as most people do. The Oxford Group, which served as a model for the AA program, proposed that people should try "surrendering as much of yourself as you understand to as much of God as you understand."[25] One of the Oxford Group principles states, "Man can only do God's will and bring himself into alignment and harmony with God's plan when he has surrendered his will, ego, and his sins to God. This is called self-surrender."[26]

In his book *A Gentle Path through the Twelve Steps*, Patrick Carnes addresses the theme of surrender and the heroic journey:

> Joseph Campbell and others who have studied the hero's myths in many lands notice that a similar process is central in every hero's journey. The hero comes to a point where he or she must stop worrying about what to do or how to overcome the obstacles in the way, and just do what needs to be done. Right action comes by taking the next step. But first the hero must surrender or submit to the teaching of a spiritual guide or mentor. Through this process, the hero learns the inner discernment necessary to make wise decisions.[27]

Here is a key. At such a turning point in a person's life, one must find a "spiritual guide or mentor" to assist with the process. Alcoholics have been fighting a lonely battle for a long time, letting no one in on the secrets of the loss of control of their lives. It is at this exact point that surrender takes place but not in solitude. People are now available and eager to help. And those who are offering to help, potential sponsors, have all trod this path themselves. And so having made a decision and armed with a sponsor, it is time to take that first step into the forest and begin the fearsome task of an honest self-examination. This brings us to step 4, but first, let us look at Niall's story.

Niall's Story

A Story of Survival

It all started when Mom decided that she had had enough of this "Catholic bullshit," as she used to call it. "They've brainwashed us into believing that we need more Catholic babies," she would cry. The rhythm method, as it used to be called, didn't work out so well for her and Mike. Five babies in just under seven years. She got a diaphragm and put it to work. Great results for almost three years. Then it was Bisno, the family dog, who must have rejoiced at finding a new chew toy. That was the end of the diaphragm. Nine months later, I appeared.

This story might seem a bit odd about how I happened to come into this world. It was the Christmas and Thanksgiving stories that seared this memory into all our minds. There was a lot of fun made at the expense of Bisno and me.

As years passed and memories started shaping in my mind, I often wondered whether my existence was a big mistake. It was all the damn dog's fault. Old Bisno was the last one down the line. The only one I could point my finger at. I sometimes wished I were not born at all. The afterbirth is how they referred to me. "You shouldn't even be here," they would say. What a great way to start a meaningful life.

Mom and Dad were in a plane crash in late 1961. They survived but barely. It threw the clan into a tumultuous time. The oldest, eleven, and me, a year and a half. Times became very tough. It was a private plane, and there was no insurance. My grandmother came to live with us, and we were getting handouts from the church and many of the neighbors. We were poor for the next several years.

I actually have a quite vivid memory of the day Mom returned home from Houston, about six weeks after the crash. From our living room window, I saw an ambulance back into our driveway. They rolled her out on a gurney and brought her to her bed. We all gathered around, and I got to climb in bed with her as she held me. These two minutes are the earliest memory I have.

When I was three or four, it had become commonplace for my dad to arrive home in one of his moods. He would be accompanied by a friend or work associate, and he would call any of the kids who were home to come into the living room. Ultimately it would be one or all three of the youngest. He would make us drop our drawers and bend over, bare-assed, and give us each a good whack with his belt. He would tell us that this was for all the things we did wrong today. We would run off screaming, and he and his buddies would stand there laughing. Eventually, when we heard the garage door opening, we would dart out the back door, jump the fence, and wait an hour or so before returning. Fear from within the walls of our home.

It was no better at St. Claire's, where I attended first and second grade. The fear was with me. One day, when class came to attention and after we pledged the flag, we were ordered to sit down. I stood next to my desk. Sister Knuckles told me to sit down in my chair. I said, "But I can't, Sister."

"Why?"

"My legs hurt."

"Why do your legs hurt"?

"My dad hit me with a coat hanger last night and it hurts."

She came over next to me, shoved me into my seat, and said, "You probably deserved it. And stop your crying, or I'll send you to see Sister Superior."

I managed to hold back my tears.

Although we all suffered at the hand of Mike, nobody was worse off than Patrick. Patrick and Mike really learned to hate each other. Patrick was around ten or eleven when he started having a problem with rather large and grotesque skid marks in his shorts. Mike figured he would be able to teach us all a lesson at the expense of Patrick. If Mom complained about Patrick leaving shitty shorts in the hamper, Mike would make him go get the skidded shorts and invert them, and he would have to wear them on his head. He would have to parade around the house,

while we all took our shots at him. After a few minutes of total humiliation, he was ordered to take the shorts in the bathroom and rinse them
out. I know this scared Patrick greatly. Twenty years later, when we
were roasting my dad on a cruise, Patrick entered the room to do his skit
with a pair of peanut butter–smeared shorts atop his head.

Patrick started to get tired of Mike's torturous ways. He began to
fight back, and fight they did. I remember one time they were in the
backyard when they started going at it. Fists flying. Blood and screams
filled the air. It was mostly me screaming, as I was sure one of them
was going to kill the other. I dared not get too close, as a wild fist might
come my way. Somebody called the police, but by the time they got
there, the commotion had halted. The incident was explained away, and
the cops left. I honestly don't ever remember a more traumatic scene in
my life. I hated my dad, too.

Mike's ideas of fatherhood seemed at the time to be what was normal. He would put Tabasco sauce on our thumbs at bedtime so we
would not suck them throughout the night. He was afraid that we would
push our teeth forward, and then when we got older, we would have to
have braces. That would cost. After a week or two, I woke up in the wee
hours screaming, with incredible burning in my eyes. Mom put an end
to the Tabasco experiment.

On occasion, Mom would leave town for a long weekend of black-
jack in Tahoe with a couple of her girlfriends, leaving Dad in charge
of the homemaking duties. He was too cheap to order takeout for such
a large crowd, so he would make us pizza for dinner. An English muf-
fin with tomato paste, topped with cheese, baked in the oven. Dinner. I
hated it when he would burn these things because we would have to eat
them anyway. All the time, he was sucking down fresh-cooked Dunge-
ness crab, which he would get from the Race Street Market on his way
home from work. We dared not ask him for even a taste, or we were
liable to get some crab shell thrown our way. Something about Dunge-
ness crab that fired up his mean streak.

I always hated it when Mom would leave. One day, the six kids
were in a particularly jovial mood at the dinner table. Dad didn't like
the noise, so he grabbed his crab in a bowl and went to the TV room.
"The next one of you to make a sound is going to get the belt." My
sister started showing me the chewed-up food in her mouth, and I
started laughing. That was it. We heard Dad getting out of the chair and

stomping out into the kitchen, drawing his belt from his waist. He knew it was me, and I knew he knew it was me. I only had time to take the fetal position in my chair, covering my head and face. He started swinging. It was the second or third strike that caught my left knee and split it open. The blood squirted, and I was screaming for my life. The other kids froze. It all stopped, and he went to the other room. I think he realized it was a bit much. The girls took me to the bathroom and patched me up. Patrick was fed up but dared not make a sound. When the table was cleared and order somewhat restored, he said, "Come with me."

We went outside and got on his bike, me on the handlebars. He said that we were going to go to the police station and show the cops what he had done. We made it to the school playground, which was on the way, and decided to think this over. We figured that, because Mom was out of town, they probably would not charge him with child abuse, and we would likely suffer an even worse beating afterward. We decided to play on the swings instead. Mom came home a couple days later, and I had to go to the hospital and get six stitches in my knee.

These are but a few of the stories of family life. It wasn't all bad all the time, just most of the time. Mike was a real Jekyll-and-Hyde dude. I know his early life was dominated by an overbearing alcoholic father, but I never understood what brought on his hatred for his own children. I know he battled his stresses and all his physical pain (he told us about that all the time—a real hypochondriac), but how could you treat anybody the way he treated us? If there was ever a man who needed to be vasectomized and left childless, it was Mike. He didn't deserve us.

The six of us all have our own disorders. Alcohol, drugs, food, sex, money, anger, depression, anxiety, self-centeredness, obsessive, compulsive, domination; did I say alcohol? I feel that I am the lucky one of the clan. I've been freed from my alcoholic condition. There are a couple of other things on the aforementioned list from which I still suffer, to a much lesser degree. I have learned that I am responsible for *my* conditions. There are many reasons for how and why I got here. I wasn't given the best start in life, but there's no blame to be given now, and the buck stops here.

I see issues in my siblings and their kids. I see some in my son. Genetics must play a bigger part than I thought. I did the best I could to stop the cycle. Maybe Mike wasn't totally to blame, but there was never any remorse. He seemed to accept it as normal, and perhaps it was through his eyes. I like my normal these days. It's the closest I think I've ever been to normal. Surviving was my normal, but now it isn't good enough to just survive.

It seems to me that there are two types of survival that I have had experience with. There is the external, and then there's internal survival. The external survival is a by-product of the forces going on outside myself—those things that we seemly have little or no control over. For me, this was the first twelve or thirteen years of life. The internal survival is what's been happening since—surviving myself and my own insanity. What worked early on as survival skills failed me completely as living skills.

And what survival skills did I acquire? What seemed to work better than anything else was intoxication. At eleven and twelve years of age, one thing was clear: Getting high helped make some sense of things and provided temporary relief. So that's what I did. Sniffing glue, stealing booze from a neighbor and from my parents, and smoking some pot when I could get it. Not a glorious beginning, but it seemed to work. I felt OK.

It was apparent to others that my actions, my decision making, and ultimately my thinking were astray. But not to me. My freshman and sophomore years were such a blur. LSD, PCP (it's the worst—don't ever let your kids do this!), as much pot as possible, occasionally some coke or crank, and can't forget the mushrooms. This was all feeding the craving for beer, which had become more available.

The problems became greater. There was a physical, legal, social, economical, and emotional price that had to be paid. It came from the skin off my back, literally. The rolled car injuring me and my friend was part of those legal issues. There was possession at a high school dance, drunk at school, and being led out of the principal's office in handcuffs. I didn't hang out with the wrong crowd—I was the wrong crowd. People saw that and were getting tired of it.

The bubble popped on July 4, 1975. It was about a week after my sixteenth birthday. The drunk started late in the morning, and it wasn't yet dark when I decided to stumble on home. Dad found me wobbling around the backyard, and like a hungry hyena, he tore into me. When I came out of the blackout, which I had been in for several hours, I was in a towel, wet, standing at the front door with my parents, talking to two Santa Clara policemen.

I had been beaten up pretty badly by my father. My mother was pleading to have me taken away. My dad was onboard, too. They were done, and I could not blame them. But I caught a break. Juvenile hall was overbooked and could not take any more guests. Big-boy jail was my only option. The police really discouraged this, for my safety. My brother, who was holding me and keeping me upright, agreed with the cops. The parents gave it some thought, and I got to stay home that night.

Sometime between 9:00 p.m., July 4, and 8:00 a.m., July 5, the decision was made (it's possible this decision was made another time, but my timely drunk pushed the envelope) for me to be sent to school in Galway, Ireland. Nothing in that household ever seemed to happen in a subtle fashion. My life to this point had been in continual chaos. Being shipped off to Ireland as a form of rehab was no exception. They sent me as far away as possible, turning me over to the Catholic brothers and priests, who would have total control and keep me in line.

I returned from Ireland with new ideas on how to handle life. I had to be much more discreet. I found that not getting caught sure helped. I was beginning to understand more about the consequences of my actions. Survival of the external was becoming survival of the internal—my self-destructive nature. Hindsight shows that, as hard as I tried to blame the world for my issues as they arose, it really was my thinking and actions that continued to haunt me. This would continue for ten more years. I'm kind of a slow learner. Then came sobriety. If I had known how hard it was going to be, I might have opted to stay drunk, die young, and live a seemingly easier life. Key word: *seemingly*!

You take a twenty-eight-year-old man with the mindset of a young teen, sober him up, and watch him go. So much like a pinball in the machine—with very active bumpers. I spent twenty-eight years honing my survival skills. Taking my best stab at life just to be told how wrong I had been. As obvious as it was to just about anybody near me, I was very much in the dark as to how a halfway decent life should be lived. I thought I had been doing OK to this point. There's two ways to think about this: Was I doing an OK job at making a decent life for myself, or was I doing a great job of surviving? Learning to survive myself would take the next thirty years.

The toughest part of my journey was probably the first twenty-five years of sobriety. The things I did to myself, the internal, which I somehow survived, would make my first twenty-five years of life pale in comparison. A bad marriage and even worse divorce. Losing nearly all my money in bad real estate deals. Losing what I felt to be true love. Losing touch with my son. Moving from Marietta, Georgia, to Tucson, Arizona, trying to be closer to my son. Then came one more of those external things, a bulging disk as a result from the "accident" I had in the first year of sobriety.

The "accident" happened at about eight months sober. A crushed pelvis, herniated disc, broken leg, and severely dislocated leg led me to a forty-eight-day hospital stay and nearly two years of physical rehab before getting back to my new normal. The external was the accident itself. A very freak dirt-bike wreck. The internal (my thinking and ultimately my decision) aspect came after listening to my brother harass me into going dirt-bike riding with him. He kept telling me what a chicken I was and that I needed to go because it would be such a good time. He was my big brother. I couldn't let him down. Bad decision.

At twenty years sober, I was ready to commit suicide. Severe pain from the bulging disk, severe sleep deprivation, and prescription opioids (taken as prescribed, with no physical effect) wore me down and gave me the feeling that there would be no end to all of this. In this very fragile state of mind, I decided that life was no longer worth living. I made a plan. I was going to drive myself off a very high cliff to end this suffering. But the miracle of my God intervening took me elsewhere.

This idea of my God is unique to me. This spiritual being knows me well. The intervention had to be in terms that I would understand. In the middle of the night, after finding my jumping-off spot, I stopped and had one last talk with God. I asked him to simply give me something, some kind of sign that I need to turn around and not do this. In the early-morning hours of a beautiful desert night, my prayer was answered. A minivan pulled up and parked about thirty feet away. It was dark. The van started making a squeaking noise, followed by the passionate moans of a woman in ecstasy. That's right—my sign was a couple having sex right there in front of me. I could not help but laugh and took that as the purest sign of my God telling me to go home, which I did. By the time the sun rose, I was talking to my AA sponsor, who guided me to a local psych ward. I asked for help, and that page was turned.

At forty-nine years old, I was about $3,000 from being broke, no job, in pain, and pretty much out of options. My mom accepted me back into her San Francisco condo, where I would reside for the next two years. It was under the guise of me being her caretaker, as she was becoming much more forgetful. She would tell her friends she was taking care of me, and I would tell my friends just the opposite. I guess it was a little of both. This was really the best two years I had ever had with her. We had such a good time, until my brother decided to rear his evil head again.

It was your typical family business being torn apart by greed, lies, and general alcoholic behavior. I managed to escape most of the following two years of lawsuits and family battles. The focus shifted from me to my sister, who had cared for the family business for twenty years. But I was out, on my own for the first time ever. My bad habit of relying on family for emergency financial support had come to an end. I managed to bounce around for a couple of years until I landed the position as a sales representative for the company I work for today. Those first few years back out on my own were particularly difficult. Likely the most difficult time I had to survive to this point in life. But I think it was what I needed to move forward on my recovery journey.

My relationship with God has gone through a lot of transition. My Catholic upbringing did nothing but scare me. But something stuck from the early days, as I can always remember, as far back as I can, that there was a God. I don't ever remember any more than this, just that God was there. I did not know what that meant. I did not know how to call on God. I did not know that God was to be the basis of my life. Simple ignorance. As much as I deluded myself into thinking that that my life was pretty smooth and in my control, hindsight clearly shows that there was a greater power at work. There had to be, or I would not have survived.

It doesn't matter whether it was a horrendous accident, awful choices in life partners, having my son taken away for a few years, really dumb financial decisions, or medical conditions so bleak that life became not worth living, there's one thing in common: God had never left my side. I would never have learned this if it were not for these nonsensical, near-laughable situations I got myself into. Every deep situation I got into in life, I've seemed to come out the other side with a better understanding of God, with a little more gratitude and a better story to share. God has truly been my saving grace.

In my Catholic upbringing, I learned of many miracles stated in the Bible. I never believed any of these happened. It was not logical. None of it made any sense until that day came when I knew my drinking days were over. A joint in one hand and a beer in the other, I put them down and asked for help. I did not know this then, but this was nothing short of a miracle. One moment enjoying a high, and the next *knowing* I'm done. It took a long time before I understood it was God's work.

Only a few months after I quit drinking and drugging came the dirt-bike accident. Nearly two months in the hospital and another eighteen months rehabbing. Losing everything (money, property, career, and physical ability), only to be brought back whole within a few years. Miracle number 2 but still not seeing it as such. But my newfound sobriety and much free time to dive into said sobriety gave me the chance to think about how God operates in my life.

I began working on my own unique understanding of how this God, dwelling within me and caring for me, can work in my life. Many years and much misunderstanding got me ever closer to the God of my understanding. With the help of Alcoholics Anonymous, great guidance, and awesome new friendships, my view of God was becoming clearer. There is no doubt that all these other people helping me on my way may actually be the very God I speak of—or at least doing His job.

The God I learned about in the AA program and from my friends, the God of my understanding, I'm convinced, wants nothing but good for me. I now expect good things to happen in my life when things are falling apart all around me. One thing I struggle with to some degree today is why it always has to be such a shit show to get a clear miraculous message from God. I think it's because God is a comedian. Kind of like a puppet master having a really good time. My God laughs at me, and that's OK.

It's been a hard time trying to figure out life. Having guidance through the twelve steps of recovery, mentors, fellowship, and the opportunity to give back has forged a clearer path—live the principles of a good life without giving it much thought. The choices I'm presented seem to be leading me ever closer to my God. I feel that this is what my recovery is all about—do whatever is necessary to build that conscious contact with God.

Chapter Five

The Inward Journey

Steps 4 and 5

STEP 4: "MADE A SEARCHING AND FEARLESS MORAL INVENTORY OF OURSELVES."[1]

Thus far, as we have seen, at every point of the heroic journey resistance and refusal is encountered. As already mentioned, the call to adventure is refused over and over, often for many years. Indeed, some never even get to the first step, that of admitting defeat. (Thus, the hero within, who is present in each of us, never has the opportunity to emerge.) Next, resistance to believing that there is another way must be overcome. Successfully overcoming this inner resistive force involves accepting help from a power greater than oneself, whatever that may mean to any given person. If one takes that step, as discussed in the previous chapter, the subsequent step is a surrender to that higher power, even if it is just to the power of the AA program—in AA parlance, a Group of Drunks (GOD).

The courage required to step into an AA room for the first time is immense and can only be found within the person who takes that step. Certainly, outside pressure is usually felt, but outside pressure has been resisted before. (A friend who had been trying for years to get sober in AA had recently married a woman who was no stranger to alcoholics or to alcoholism. One day, she had reached her limit with his drinking. She told him to get to a meeting that same day and not to come home without the phone number of a sponsor. Seeing no alternative, he followed instructions and has not had a drink for more than twenty years.)

Somehow, someway, a decision to give AA a try (or another try) has been made. A directory of AA meetings has been consulted, or a call to AA has been made, and a time and place has been decided on.

Once inside the room, a person is warmly greeted, and a process of introduction to the recovery program begins. Seeing so many seemingly happy, contented people at the meeting is surprising and comforting. The meeting begins; a section from the Big Book, which includes the twelve steps, is read; announcements are made; and members begin to share their experience, strength, and hope. Now the courage summoned to get to the meeting is rewarded by the appearance of success demonstrated by the people in the room. What comes next on this journey?

We all know (or most of us do) that we have a dark side. We experience thoughts or are tempted to do things that cause us to feel shame if we admit these things to ourselves. Dr. Carl Jung devoted much of his career to the study of the human personality. He described several components or structures that together comprise this totality, or psyche, as he called it. I mentioned this in chapter 1. Here I focus on two such structures to illustrate the dilemma of the fourth step.

The outermost aspect of the personality Jung calls the persona. This is the mask that we wear; it is what we present to the outside world. For that matter, it is also what we present to ourselves. It is who we see in the mirror. However, as discussed earlier, it is commonly understood that there are aspects of our lives that we are only dimly aware of, if at all. We can refer to this aspect of ourselves as our unconscious. According to Dr. Jung, there are many components to the unconscious. The aspect of the unconscious I focus on at this time is what he called the shadow.

As Murray Stein puts it, "The shadow is the image of ourselves that slides along behind us as we walk toward the light."[2] We may be only vaguely aware that we cast a shadow, that we have a dark side that is unshakeable—that there is more to ourselves than we understand. Indeed, sometimes others can see our shadows even if we think we are projecting nothing but sunlight and bluebirds. And the better people know us, the less we can hide. Regarding his own frustration, St. Paul said, "For I know that good itself does not dwell within me, that is, in my sinful nature. For I have the desire to do what is good, but I cannot carry it out. For I do not do the good I want to do, but the evil I do not want to do—this I keep on doing."[3] For St. Paul, the dark side, in his terminology, is his *sinful nature*. He says that because of his "dark side," without God's help, he cannot be the best person that he can be.

According to Dr. Jung, the goal of psychological development is the integration of the various components of the personality. People with addictions have failed to progress in such development because they have used drugs, alcohol, or mood-altering behaviors to avoid dealing with the challenges presented in their lives. Personality integration hinges on self-acceptance, which will never happen until one takes an honest stock of oneself. And this won't happen until the individual becomes convinced that there is no other option than to move forward with this task. And according to the Coptic Gospel of Thomas, "Jesus said, 'If you give birth to what's within you, what you have within you will save you. If you don't have that within you, what you don't have within you will kill you.'"[4]

According to Murray Stein, the personal history and characteristics of which one is ashamed are often felt to be "radically evil . . . [however] frequently shadow material is not evil. It is only felt to be so because of the shame attached to it due to its nonconformity with the persona."[5] Thinking about it this way, one might expect an honest self-appraisal to yield at least a passing grade, higher than what would have been projected before starting the process, and it could be immensely liberating.

When a hero accepts the call, he or she is told that, even though the challenge appears impossible to complete, help will be given. This help can be of a divine or spiritual nature, such as the ten plagues that God visited on the Egyptians to secure the release of the Hebrew people from the grip of Pharaoh. Sometimes it comes in the form of a guide, such as in Dante's *Divine Comedy* (the hero in this epic had two guides, first Virgil and then Beatrice). In addiction recovery, there is the program itself with the twelve steps spelled out, but it also includes guidance from those who have already walked the walk. Successful navigation of the twelve steps is typically done with the aid of a sponsor, and nowhere in the journey is the sponsor more needed than the fourth step. It is precisely at this point that many travelers step off the path, refuse the call, stop calling their sponsor, fail to attempt or fail to complete the fourth step, and sooner or later resume their addictive behaviors.

While there are instructions in the Big Book for doing the fourth step, including a chart to help organize the task, one hardly knows where or how to begin. The job seems overwhelming. People are, on the one hand, at a loss for what to say and, on the other hand, feel as though, once they start, they will produce a tragic novel of one thousand pages. Without a sponsor—a person who has already done the fourth step with the assistance of his or her sponsor and who likely has taken others through the process while acting as their sponsor—the task will probably be done incompletely or possibly not at all.

One of the remarkable things about AA is the trust that quickly develops between people. Newcomers may find themselves disclosing long-held secrets to someone they met only days or weeks previously. Sponsors will suggest a process of inventory taking based on their own experiences and consistent with the AA program. If the suggestions are followed, the job will be completed in a reasonable amount of time. Initiates into the program will discover that they are neither as good as they made themselves out to be nor as bad as they feared. The inventory does not have to be done perfectly; indeed, it never will be. The point is to do it—and to do it with guidance.

It is with this step that it becomes clear that there are, in reality, two heroic journeys that go on at the same time. The first and most immediately to the point is going through each day without slipping back into addictive behaviors. The addict must abstain in the real world where temptations abound, whether it is exposure to gatherings where people are drinking or getting high, the advertisements on television, or the beer or video poker machines at the convenience store. The recovering person must change because the rest of the world is not going to. And of course, the recovering person may have cravings that seem to have no external trigger; the obsession may not have yet been entirely removed.

The second and simultaneous journey is the interior one—the journey of self-discovery. Such a journey would be impossible while in the grip of active addiction. Although nobody coming into recovery has such a journey of self-discovery on their wish list, it turns out to be the more meaningful and rewarding of the two. It leads to what the program refers to as a "spiritual awakening," an unimaginable goal at the outset.

People who are just entering into a recovery process have a lot of guilt on their conscience. There are things that bother them that they have never disclosed, indeed, things that they have sworn to themselves that would never be revealed. So the fourth step includes some items that carry a good deal of shame and guilt. As important as it may be to be thorough and not leave anything of this sort out, most of the inventory is less emotionally taxing.

As a way of organizing the task and ensuring thoroughness, some format is suggested. In his writings, Bill Wilson frequently refers to "defects of character" and "shortcomings." One can, with the help of a sponsor, make such a list and then list the corresponding character asset in an opposite column of a page. Then one can write about where they see themselves on the continuum for each pair. For example, one can list "impatience" on one side of the ledger and "patience" on the other and then write examples about where they see themselves on that continuum. In this manner, the exercise will be balanced and representative of who the person actually is or has been.

The inward journey is a quest for self-knowledge, but it is more than that. It is a spiritual quest. Referring again to Dr. Jung and his theory of the personality, the deepest level is what he called the self. Try not to be confused with the terminology. It is at this point that the person and God experience spiritual union. The ultimate goal of the heroic journey is to fuse our spirit with God's *in our awareness*, the spiritual awakening referred to in step 12. The fourth step is a major step in this direction. Having completed one's best effort, it is time to proceed with the fifth step.

STEP 5: "ADMITTED TO GOD, TO OURSELVES, AND TO ANOTHER HUMAN BEING THE EXACT NATURE OF OUR WRONGS."[6]

As Vernon J. Bourke wrote nearly a century ago, "Nearly every man has one story which burns within him until it is told."[7] Too many people never tell their story or never tell it in a manner that quenches the fire. Many alcoholics will, under the influence of alcohol, begin a morose tale of tragedy and suffering that they have experienced under conditions of great hardship or danger. It is the same story every time and may even be true. But there is no progression to a resolution of their pain, hatred, or self-loathing. Such a tale told in an inebriated state is usually focused on harms done by others. Rarely does one look at his or her own part in such an altered state. It is a tale saturated with resentment and self-pity.

The guidance received on the heroic journey includes the requirement of being honest with others but especially being honest with oneself. In fact, the book *Alcoholics Anonymous* states that the only people who fail at the program of recovery are those who are "constitutionally incapable of being honest with themselves."[8] It does *not* say constitutionally incapable of being honest with others or with God. The temptation must be overcome to skip over certain events of the past, certain secrets of which we are ashamed, or to fail to acknowledge certain weaknesses of our character. At every step of the journey, heroes are challenged to do what seems to be more than they can manage.

Much courage is required, and if the effort is to be successful, then they must place reliance on a higher power. Ironically, those who believe in God will find that, even though they would prefer to hide certain things from God, it is through reliance on Him that one can summon the courage to open up and make these admissions. There may be a temptation to think, "Well, God knows everything anyway, so why bother with this step?" This is part of the reason another trusted person must be involved.

Another reason to involve another person is that our fears of being judged will not be realized. Our partner in this step, typically either a sponsor or a clergyperson, will listen thoughtfully, give encouragement, say that they have heard all this before, and may have even done most of it themselves in the past. But the best reason to do the fifth step is that it is part of the program, and people who design their own recovery journey have placed the responsibility for the success of their recovery in the hands of their darker selves. AA wisdom holds that it is our secrets that keep us sick. And a secret confessed only to God remains a secret.

I make one cautionary point about the selection of the right person to hear the fifth step. The courts have held that an AA sponsor, as such, does not have immunity from testifying in court about what he or she has been told. Many states also do not extend the privilege of immunity to professional addiction counselors. Individuals whose "confessions" include crimes for which they could be prosecuted should do at least this part of their fifth step with a person who will be able to keep the confidence under all conditions. Such a person would be either one's physician, attorney, or a clergyperson. In such a situation, the hero may take part of the fifth step with one person and another part of the step with another person. Whichever approach is taken, it is important to not procrastinate in completing the step.

A great benefit of doing the fifth step is that it opens people in recovery to full participation in life as a member of the human race. Notice that the step does not say that we admit our wrongs. Rather, it says we admit the "*exact nature* of our wrongs."[9] In wondering why this phrase was used by Bill Wilson, a possible explanation is that the *exact nature* referred to is our *human nature*. (I credit my wife, Judy Gordon, for pointing this out to me.) In fact, the discovery of ourselves in our humanity at depth is where we are going on our journey. Completion of this step is an accomplishment. The hero has arrived at a destination on the heroic journey.

The rewards are usually immediate and profound. In *Alcoholics Anonymous*, the experience is described as follows:

> Once we have taken this step, withholding nothing, we are delighted. We can look the world in the eye. We can be alone at perfect peace and ease. Our fears fall from us. We begin to feel the nearness of our Creator. We may have had certain spiritual beliefs, but now we begin to have a spiritual experience. The feeling that the drink problem has disappeared will often come strongly. We feel we are on the Broad Highway, walking hand in hand with the Spirit of the Universe.[10]

Notice the use of language of journeying. Our heroes have arrived at a point where they have experienced the complete exposure and deflation of their hyperinflated egos, hyperinflated to cover up the deep sense of inferiority and inadequacy that they have unjustifiably felt for their entire lives. They discover that their inadequacy is a lie told by others but mostly told by themselves. Now, in partnership with their higher power, they can continue the journey into a new life of recovery, finally able to have compassion for themselves and for their fellow man.

As pointed out in *Twelve Steps and Twelve Traditions*, a consequence of taking the fifth step is "we shall get rid of that terrible sense of isolation we've always had."[11] By going through this difficult and painful process, heroes are purged of self-hate and inner demons. They come to realize that they are like other people, no better and no worse. They realize that all people are on life's journey, having daily adventures, being in relationships with others, making their own contributions to improving the world, and continuing to follow a spiritual path.

While heroes may not give themselves permission to take a pat on the back and take a rest from the quest, they certainly can take satisfaction in what has been accomplished thus far, and with gratitude be motivated to push onward in the hopeful expectation that, with continued progress, more rewards will come. And heroes cannot lose sight of the fact that, if a big time-out is taken from the journey, alcohol is patiently waiting. Once again, the temptation to refuse to continue with the journey may arise, but heroes cannot take a vacation from it.

Hawk's Story

Traveling the Red Road

Our stories disclose in a general way what we were like, what happened, and what we are like now. What was I like? I was a man full of fear, pretending to have it all together. Some of the fear was real, some imagined. The real fear came from my upbringing of not having enough food or rent money, being evicted, and parents being arrested for bad checks, to name a few. I am the third of seven kids: two older brothers and one younger, all within one year of each other, and three sisters spaced about four years apart.

We grew up in Southern California around the horse racetracks, as our dad was a horse trainer. He had a temper and liked to drink and bet on the horses and was not around that much. Mom was addicted to him and his pie-in-the-sky attitude toward life and followed him all over the country. We moved twenty-two times in nineteen years; one move was next door to the place we were living. We passed furniture and everything over the fence!

We moved from California to Virginia with a U-Haul trailer full of our junk. Dad, Mom, three brothers, two sisters, our family cocker spaniel, and Dad's favorite fighting chicken named Grey Boy. We stayed one summer only to go back to Southern California. We did it again a few years later but without the dog or chicken. They had passed on. A few years later, we drove to Chicago because Dad was there at a racetrack, and Mom suspected that he was having an affair, so off we went. We were back in California by winter. Crazy things happened all the time, and I did not recognize them for how crazy they were while in the middle of it all.

Sometimes, when Dad was not showing up or sending money, we gathered soft drink bottles from the roadside and cashed them in for flour and baking powder so mom could make bread or pancakes for dinner. We lived in Northern California for a while, and we got good at following the vegetable trucks coming from the fields, as they would drop a box of lettuce or cabbage when they hit a pothole in the road. We could buy beans and rice in bulk at the local swap meets.

I always felt different and like an outsider every time we moved to a different school. The kids all knew each other and had grown up together. Just as I began to make friends, we would move again. We usually lived in a run-down place on the outskirts of town on the wrong side of the tracks, which did not help with making friends. I felt different because I *was* different.

When I was twelve or thirteen, we were staying in a ramshackle house on a small farm. The owner gave a party for his rich friends, and there was a keg of beer. That was the first time I drank, and I loved the change that came over me. I took empty milk bottles, filled them with beer, and hid them under my bed. I drank warm flat beer for three days. My brothers did not.

At age seventeen, I was awakened by my oldest brother, David, pulling me out of my bunk out into the yard. I had passed out and vomited into my pillow and the noise woke him up. That was the first time he saved my life. I later discovered that I had been driving in the foothills of Pasadena in our Ford Ranchero in a complete blackout with three or four other guys, only knew one of them, after we had stolen some booze from a local liquor store. The one kid I knew relayed the story to me the next day.

I did not drink every day, but I drank as often as I could. I was still in high school but would get up at 5:00 a.m. to work on the racetrack walking the racehorses after they exercised. That got me enough money to buy booze and to help with buying food.

In 1966, I bought a 1955 Ford station wagon, rebuilt the engine, and drove from California to Louisville with my brother Bill, Mom, and three sisters. Dad was at Churchill Downs, so I worked there for a while and then got a job as a maintenance man at an apartment complex. They gave me an apartment as part of my pay, and I started drinking every day after work.

The drinking got me fired, and I got drafted right after I gave my change of address to the draft board. I took my basic training at Fort Knox, so my brother (or mom) would bring a bottle of booze and my girlfriend over to visit often. I turned twenty-one while in advanced training in Arizona, which did not make much of a difference to my drinking habit. I got orders to go to Germany. I missed Vietnam by pure luck. When I got to Germany, I figured out a way to get very cheap booze from the Army liquor store. It was not legal, but I had learned a lot from my parents. I also found many other forms of recreational substances that changed the way I felt.

After two years, I returned to Louisville and got even with the girl I had dated a few years earlier; I married her. That only lasted two years. She spent a year of that time in a Kentucky mental hospital. I did not handle that very well. I drank and smoked my way through all the emotions as they came up. After our divorce I dated several ladies and continued to party nonstop.

I had started my own remodeling business and decided it was time for a change of latitude. I moved to Sarasota, Florida, thinking that I would not drink as much being away from all the negative events in Louisville. So I guess I was starting to admit to myself that my drinking was a problem. Moving did not work. I continued to lose money, lose friends, lose customers, all due to daily drinking. I tried all the formulas to stop, but nothing worked. I hid my drinking from my new wife for about a year. Things got bad, so I decided to move to Atlanta and work for my brother Bill remodeling homes. I left my wife to do all the work of packing and moving. Rude!

We were in Atlanta about one year and bought a house (I have no idea how she did that), and I went back to working for myself, as Bill had just about given up on me being drunk all the time. I was getting sick to my stomach every morning and would get out the door to the woods next door to throw up so my wife would not see just how sick I was.

The last day of drinking I was too sick to keep the morning vodka down. My body had had all it could take. In my basement, I had a grand mal seizure, causing me to crash and hit my head on the concrete floor. By the grace of God, my brother David was there that morning to help with a project. He stuffed rags on my head to stop the bleeding and called 911. I woke up strapped to a gurney in Smyrna Hospital, not having a clue what had happened. I stayed there for five days of IV detox before I was released to go into a rehab hospital that my wife had arranged for me.

She was done with the whole thing, and I did not blame her. If I did not stop drinking, she was gone. Period. The rehab introduced me to Alcoholics Anonymous meetings, which I have attended ever since. I did what was suggested and told to do by other members who had stayed sober for long periods of time. Some even had more than a year of not drinking and were happy people!

In early recovery, I was desperate to find a higher power because I was told I needed one to stay sober. My sponsor suggested I not try so hard and "let it come to you." Shortly after my second year of sobriety, I was attending a spiritual renewal workshop in Northern California, and one of the experiences offered was a Native American sweat lodge ceremony (Inipi in the Lakota language).

I participated in the construction of the lodge, gathering the firewood, gathering and placing the stones on the fire, and listening to the leader explain the history of the ceremony. The stones were heated for three hours, and then it was time to enter the lodge. The stones were brought in a few at a time, and when the flap (door) was closed, it was pitch black, except for the glow of the red-hot stones. Water was poured over the rocks as songs were sung to the beating of a drum. The heat became nearly unbearable.

After a few minutes, the flap was opened, and more stones brought in. This was done four times with drinking water offered each time. During the third round, I felt the sweat dripping from me onto the ground, and I saw the water penetrating down into Mother Earth, making its way to the nearby stream, then to the river, then to the ocean, where it evaporated and became rain that fell on me and became the sweat that was pouring from me. The endless cycle of all things became clear to me, and I *felt* the presence of a power greater than myself. I knew I was part of the power of the universe. That feeling has stayed with me since that day.

As we were leaving the workshop location to return to Atlanta, the lodge leader, Thunder Bear, received a "message" that he was to teach me the way of the sacred pipe. So I went to his place in South Carolina on the weekends for the next year and learned the proper way to conduct the Chanupa ceremony with honor and respect. Since then, I have conducted hundreds of Chanupa ceremonies, participated in dozens of Inipi ceremonies, and been a Sun Dance supporter.

Recovery has opened my eyes to so many things that I was once blind to. I am grateful that I have the opportunity to show people another way to pray. Working the twelve steps as outlined in our AA literature, I have been able to lose the fear that once consumed every aspect of my life. I am able to help others with their recovery, participate in life on life's terms, and feel truly content. My wife and I have now been married forty years, and she has chosen the twelve step way of life, as well. The promises mentioned after step 9 in the AA Big Book continue to come true as I work for them each day.

Chapter Six

Transformation

Steps 6 and 7

STEP 6: "WERE ENTIRELY READY TO HAVE GOD REMOVE ALL THESE DEFECTS OF CHARACTER."[1]

As our heroes have progressed on their journey thus far, certain discoveries have been made. Our heroes are addicts, meaning control has been lost over substance use or a behavior, with the result that the heroes' lives have become something of a disaster. Our heroes have decided that help from a higher power is necessary and could be effective. A decision has been made to surrender their will and life to the care of this higher power. A thorough self-examination has been completed, and the results shared with God and another human being. Our heroes have become members of a recovering community, pursuing the same goal of recovery in the same manner. And the realization has been made that in the process of all these discoveries and change in life practices, they have stopped drinking, drugging, gambling, or whatever the case may be.

In terms of the heroic journey, we see that our heroes have been called to the quest, refused many times, suffered longer, finally accepted the call, found a spiritual guide and direction, and until this point accomplished the quest of arresting the addiction. A journey has been made day by day through life, in much the same world in which the heroes have lived before, but now they have stopped the self-destructive behaviors that heretofore had been uncontrollable. At the same time, a journey has commenced into the interior person, and a thorough self-examination and confession of shortcomings has been made. As the result of all this, sobriety has become established, and self-esteem has improved. There is hope for a better life.

But the journey is far from over. Indeed, it is starting to dawn on the heroes that the journey never ends. It is too early in the process to dwell on this, though. Our heroes are at the precise point at which another decision must be made. The first decision was to try the twelve step process of recovery. The second decision was to surrender one's will and life over to the care of a higher power. The decision to risk a thorough self-appraisal and honestly sharing their truth with another person and God has been made. Now our heroes must decide whether they want to be a better person or not.

Frankly, this was not on the original wish list. At the outset, all the alcoholics agreed to do is quit drinking by trying the program. Seldom had they read ahead and seriously contemplated what territory was being breached. And even if the twelve steps had been read through, steps 6 and 7 seemed like something one could easily skip over, as they are followed by tasks that at first appear to be far more dangerous and intimidating: the making of amends to others.

It is easy to imagine how the contemplation of amends making could overwhelm any thought of what steps 6 and 7 seem to require. In fact, a casual reading of the Big Book suggests exactly that: One could glide right through these steps. In the 164 pages that describe the AA program, only one short paragraph is devoted to each of these steps. This business of being entirely ready to be the best possible person is where we encounter the refusal of the call once again.

It is a much more subtle challenge than the need to halt a raging addiction. Drugs, compulsive shopping, and drinking have caused devastating problems that called for drastic action and immediate relief. The heroes at one point enjoyed the effects of these addictive behaviors, but this was before they became self-destructive. When it comes to the defects of character like impatience, lust, and selfishness, they may still appear to serve an enjoyable or useful purpose. If our heroes are selfish, then they take what they want. If they are impatient, they can take it right away and get mad if they are denied. Lust is a natural human experience, even if never acted on inappropriately. And what is wrong with checking out the cute guys or gals we encounter in our daily lives?

As I wrote that last sentence, I recalled a short story I read in college, "The Girls in Their Summer Dresses" by Irwin Shaw (1913–1984). It was a fine story, and it made me think for the first time about what might be wrong with girl-watching behavior, especially by someone who is already in a relationship. But one may think, that even though it might not be the most commendable behavior, maybe it isn't really that bad, and maybe our hero isn't ready to abandon this pleasurable activity.

A friend in his second year of recovery began attending an AA meeting with a step-study format. Each week, the group read aloud from the book *Twelve Steps and Twelve Traditions*. A discussion would follow. Given the strict adherence to a one-hour meeting, the lengthy chapter on the twelfth step was split into two segments, so that over a span of thirteen weeks, the group would have read and discussed each of the twelve steps; then they would repeat the process. Over the course of a year, they would have gone through the book four times. So four times every year, if not at other times, as well, my friend was in the position of considering his level of willingness to let go of his defects of character.

After five or six years of regular attendance, one night while sitting at the meeting and listening to the discussion, it occurred to him that he had always thought of certain of his so-called defects of character as *assets* of character. If he was selfish, then he could take the biggest slice of cake. If he was impatient, then he could demand results immediately and be rude if he didn't get his demands met. If he was lustful, then he could eye the beautiful women he encountered.

However, he also realized for the first time, sitting there in that meeting, that these cherished characteristics of his were impediments to his spirituality. They came between himself and God. That night, this appeared to our friend to be a problem that demanded a solution. And it was that night that he found himself entirely ready to release these shortcomings. He decided the cost was not worth it. He wanted to stop keeping God at arm's length.

There are at least two points in this story that are worthy of note. The first is that it illustrates the typical course of recovery on this heroic journey, which is that it is a slow process. People do not achieve an advanced level of spiritual growth overnight. However, my friend in this story had stayed sober during this entire time and was making the effort day by day. The other noteworthy point is that he had his revelation while attending an AA meeting. This underscores the importance of meeting attendance for those on their journey. Every meeting, every talk with a sponsor or sponsee, every reading of the literature, and every act of service to those in need add to the reservoir of spirituality that feeds and supports people on their heroic quest.

The sixth step will never be done perfectly. It states an ideal to strive for. It becomes clear to the heroes as they walk their walk day by day that this is a step that needs to be revisited each day of the journey. The heroes have arrived at a crucial juncture in their travels. It is at this point that the realization is made that, indeed, this journey is no longer just about drinking or not drinking but also about traveling the interior spiritual path. As it says in *Twelve Steps and Twelve Traditions*, "This is the exact point at which we abandon limited objectives, and move towards God's will for us."[2] And it is time for the next challenge.

STEP 7: "HUMBLY ASKED HIM TO REMOVE OUR SHORTCOMINGS."[3]

This is the second time in the twelve step journey that the travelers discover their need for divine intervention. Our heroes have been unable and will forever be unable to stay away from a drink, a drug, a bet, a porn site, a shopping channel, and so on without the help of a higher power. Now the heroes discover that once again they are confronted with an impossible solo task. They cannot advance toward being the very best person they can be without God's help.

Remember, the shadow slithers along behind us as we walk toward the light. The human failings are rooted too deeply in *human nature*. The heroes have come to the point of recognizing that all the defects of character, including those they relied on for both survival and gratification, had to go. They had been put in the position of having to *trust* that taking this step will make them a better person contributing to a better world. But where can they get the courage to take this enormous step?

Nothing could feel more unnatural than to release all their survival skills, all their old means of self-gratification. They are being called on to be truly heroic. An important source of strength and encouragement is that it is part of the program, and they see that countless others have taken this step and not only survived but also seem to have profited from doing so. Through their acquaintanceship with many admirable and happy people in recovery, they gradually *experience* the truth that the recovery program really works.

Earlier, the heroes had *come to believe* that a higher power could restore them to sanity. Over the ensuing days, weeks, and months, this had become a reality. Now it is time to return to this source of power and take it to the next level, that of another, deeper surrender. In their reflection on what they have gained from the preceding steps, they are able to make another decision to *trust* their higher power. The heroes' courage comes from faith in the reality, availability, and effectiveness of a power greater than themselves. On their journey through their experiences thus far, they find themselves growing in hope, faith, and belief in themselves and in the process, and they begin to *trust* that, if they continue this path, the outcome will be more than they had hoped for, beyond their wildest dreams.

The heroes on their journey toward their core have come to realize that their self-improvement program has its limitations. Stephanie Covington makes the point that heroes must acknowledge to themselves that they are "responsible for the process of change in my life, *but I'm not in control of it.*"[4] Their higher power is going to have to be called on when their best efforts have failed. As Father Francis Kelly Nemeck and Marie Theresa Coombs say in their remarkable book *O Blessed Night*, "God himself must directly prune us in our depths. Moreover, that deeper purification happens not as a punishment, but in love: 'solely because of his love.'"[5] They draw their wisdom from the Bible verse that says, "I am the true vine, and my Father is the gardener. He cuts off every branch in me that bears no fruit, while every branch that does bear fruit he prunes so that it will be even more fruitful."[6] If our heroes risk being "pruned at depth," then they will make progress on their journeys.

By admitting to their not-God-ness, they open up the path to a deeper relationship with God; their fellow man; and, most of all, themselves at their core. The hero has been challenged to *"humbly ask God to remove his shortcomings."* Why are they asked to humble themselves to make this request? In truth, if the request is not made in an attitude of humility, then it is not a sincere request. Alcoholics who have come this far on their heroic journey of recovery know that they needed the help of a higher power.

The relationship with the higher power has by this time made it clear to the heroes that the power is, indeed, *higher* than they are. From this acknowledgment of the nature of their relationship with the higher power, our heroes can take the next step. Our heroes have progressed in many aspects on their journeys: from drunk to sober, from self-hate toward self-love, from isolation to having friends, from spiritual bankruptcy toward spiritual awareness, and from raging arrogance toward humility. It is now time in our trek through these pages to look at humility in greater depth.

In *Twelve Steps and Twelve Traditions*, Bill Wilson states categorically that *humility is the essential ingredient* in the twelve step journey. He says,

> The attainment of greater humility is the foundation principle of each of AA's Twelve Steps. For without some degree of humility, no alcoholic can stay sober at all. Nearly all of AAs have found, too, that unless they develop much more of this precious quality than may be required just for sobriety, they still haven't much chance of becoming truly happy. Without it, they cannot live to much useful purpose, or, in adversity, be able to summon the faith that can meet any emergency.[7]

Humility is a quality of self-estimation in relationship to others. Humble people have learned to appreciate their uniqueness without confusing it with being special. Many people have a low opinion of humility, confusing it with humiliation. Humility refers to a state of modesty, self-effacement, a lack of attachment to one's personal importance relative to others. Humiliation is a sense of shame in the face of one's behavior, appearance, or origins when such knowledge is made public. It is doubtful that truly humble people could be subject to humiliation because of their not taking themselves too seriously.

Authors who write about the twelve step journey in the recovery from addictions place much importance on the quality of humility as a personal characteristic that is essential to acquire and develop. As noted earlier, Ernest Kurtz in *Not-God* writes, "Dr. [Harry M.] Tiebout . . . recognized 'four elements . . . as playing an essential role' in the AA program: 'hitting bottom, surrender, ego reduction, and maintenance of humility.' . . . He wrote 'The specific part of the personality which must surrender is the inflated ego . . . the carry-over of infantile traits into adult life . . . a feeling of omnipotence.'"[8] It is noteworthy that Dr. Tiebout's four elements occur in sequence. First, the humiliation of complete defeat by the addiction; next, a surrender to a higher power;

then, letting go of the infantile sense of omnipotence and specialness; and finally, attainment of humility.

A good way of thinking about humility is as the place of an individual in relation to God. Humility requires assuming one's *right place* in the relationship. Ernest Kurtz calls his work on the history of AA *Not-God* because of the importance placed on alcoholics giving up the notion that they have Godlike powers. They are not in control. As they say in AA about hitting bottom, "It was my best thinking that got me here."

St. Therese of Lisieux said that "genuine holiness is a matter of enduring our imperfections patiently."[9] Implicit in that statement is that we can't wish away or get rid of our defects of character. They are part of our human nature. Also suggested in her statement is that, if God removes them, He may do so slowly. This is a task much more complicated and difficult than God removing the obsession and compulsion of one's addictions. This has been done for millions of people. So far as I know, nobody on the twelve step path has been made perfect. As travelers on the heroic journey will not be made perfect, neither will they encounter others who are perfect. This gets us to another important aspect of humility: that of not comparing oneself to others. As Kurtz and Ketcham say, "A humility that is based on the acceptance of self as imperfect will not be interested in judging others."[10]

Martin Buber in *Hasidism and Modern Man* says that, as people travel a spiritual path through their lives, acquiring virtue, the closer they attain to a high level of positive attributes, the more they realize that they are no more than one part of the family of man. He refers to this participation in the human community as the *mystery of humility*. In speaking further about this, he says, "Every man has a light over him, and when the souls of two men meet, the two lights join each other and from them there goes forth one light. And this is called generation. To feel the universal generation as a sea and oneself as a wave, that is the mystery of humility."[11]

Rabbi Yitzchak Meltzan (1854–1916) says,

Our sages teach: Humility is the pathway to peace. Strive to purify yourself of jealousy, resentment, and competition for honor. These lead to arguments and strife between people. A quiet and contented spirit—rooted in gratitude for what we possess—will be at peace. Thus, after our prayer for peace, we ask, "Before all human beings, let humility be my stance."[12]

This is the wisdom that connects heroes with others on his travels.

Humility also connects the hero with God. Rabbi Abraham Joshua Heschel says, "In reverence, suffering, and humility we discover our existence and find the bridge that leads from existence to God."[13] It is remarkable that, when all the heroes wanted to do was quit drinking or sometimes not even that but just learn to control their drinking, they found themselves on such a journey. It is remarkable that so many "ordinary drunks" could find themselves on such a quest and find themselves on the way to self-love and to the finding of the divine deep within themselves.

Each of the twelve steps contributes to the development of such a humble attitude, without which no progress can be made. Steps 1, 2, and 3 introduce the heroes to the experience of humility. They go from a position of being an expert at everything except being able to manage their lives and control their addiction to a person who has the glimmer of an idea that there is a different and better way to try living—and then to a person who has decided to try this new way. Our heroes have stopped being the "Great I Am" and started to believe that maybe their lives could be saved and were worth saving. Imagine the insanity of living as though one is at the same time the master of the universe and the lowest piece of whale dung at the bottom of the ocean. I suspect that, for many readers, this will be all too easy to imagine.

Steps 4 and 5 further the journey of self-discovery, and while the scenery is frequently unattractive, the heroes begin to see the possibility of being an acceptable human being, fit for membership in the human race. Steps 6 and 7 advance the heroes to a new and totally unexpected aspect of the journey: that of self-respect and self-love in the process of character building. As I move on and look at the remaining steps, I show how, with each step along the way, our heroes have the opportunity to grow in humility in their relationships with man, God, and self.

Youngblood's Story

Rough Beginnings

I'm going to start at the beginning, when I was brought into this world. This may seem like the natural place to start, but I prefer to avoid the topic altogether. Unfortunately, in order to give you a clear picture of the ideas and beliefs I carried throughout most of my life, I have to paint a picture of what my childhood was like.

I was put up for adoption when I was two days old; my birth mother referred to me as a "tumor that had to be removed." My adopted parents are good Christian people; they go to church all the time; put God above all else; and refuse to see the truth, no matter how clear it is. Because of this, they allowed me to be abused for more than twelve years. I believe that my parents did the best they could, the best they were capable of, and I do not fault them for the decisions they made. For a long time, I experienced a lot of hate and placed a lot of blame on the circumstances that put me into that home.

On my journey thus far, I have done a lot of work to heal and grow from the pain I have experienced. The only reason I find any of this worth mentioning is because I want you to understand the internal condition I was up against since as early as I can remember: the loneliness, fear, disgust, mistrust, and utter lack of faith in the world and its people. It was me against the world, and I was a victim to some of the worst of what humanity has to offer. These are the beliefs that drove me and controlled my decisions for a very, very long time.

I was a very gifted kid, intellectually and athletically. I was always awkward socially, but I could hide it well as long as I was in the spotlight. I learned quickly to smile, keep my head down, and not cause trouble. I learned to bottle any emotions because no one cared anyways. I learned that the easiest way to survive was to pretend that everything was fine. This worked fairly well until high school, and then I began to slowly unravel.

My first suicide attempt was at sixteen years old. I was involuntarily admitted, held for a week or so, and picked up by my parents, and life went on as though nothing had happened. Shortly after, I discovered weed for the first time. The freedom and peace that I felt after that first joint was a feeling I never wanted to lose. I was still able to keep up my grades and athletics, but nothing mattered more than being able to party and change the way that I felt. Until graduation, I smoked and drank as often as I possibly could.

I began dating other girls in high school, in secret until senior year. I lived in a small rural town with Southern Baptist parents, and it had been made very clear my entire life that homosexuality was wrong, and I would go to hell if I was gay. I met a girl who helped me see that that wasn't true, and I proudly came out at school my last year. The day before I left for college, I finally told my parents and got the reaction I expected; they didn't speak to me for months after that night. I only lasted one semester in college; I was living in downtown Atlanta with my girlfriend, getting wasted every night, discovering more party drugs and only being content when I was using some drug to change the way I felt. At the beginning of my second semester, I tried to kill myself for the second time. I believe that this was the beginning of the end, but I never could have known that then.

I withdrew from school for medical reasons and began working full-time in Atlanta. My ex, whom I could never stay away from, was doing cocaine one night, and I'd be damned if I was going to miss out on the fun. I remember she told me, "Don't do it. You have an addictive personality, and this won't end well." I laughed, brushed it off, did way too much coke, and fell in love with this powder the way I had never loved anything before. I was alive, I was strong, and I was pissed the f— off. The next couple of years are a blur of fights, anger, and self-righteous indignation for anything that got in my way. All I cared about was pissing off anyone who disapproved or disagreed with me; me against the world, remember?

When I was twenty, I met a girl who inevitably would bring me to my knees. I entered into a relationship that became violent; dangerous; abusive; and, most importantly, centered around heroin. I will never forget the way that I felt the first time I used that drug. It was the one and only time I had ever felt so safe, calm, and happy. It cured my mind of every racing thought, every painful memory, and every scar I ever had. Of course, the scars to come, the pain and destruction I caused as I chased that feeling, nothing justified what I became. But I lost control before I ever knew I had it, and the next couple of years were the worst of my life.

As a heroin addict, I stole, I lied, I manipulated, I became everything a junkie is assumed to be. I was fired from a job, became a missing person, was homeless, was disowned, and became a career criminal to feed my addiction. I could tell you a hundred stories about people I hurt, crimes I committed, the things I did wrong. The most important part of this era of my life, though, by far, is the hopelessness and misery I felt every time I opened my eyes. Always wishing I hadn't, always wishing to just fall asleep and never wake up.

When I was on the run from police and a warrant, I prayed to get pulled over driving so I could die, suicide by cop. I daydreamed of overdosing intentionally, thought up a million ways to kill myself. The loneliness one feels when there is no reason to live, no desire to breathe, but being too afraid or too cowardly to find a way out is an indescribable experience. The last time that I was locked up, I finally had the plan, the courage, and the way out. But the universe had other plans for me.

Let me tell you what I thought about God; I hated Him, thought He was a cheap f—ing bastard, didn't want anything to do with this idea of the God that I was raised with. Any "supreme being" who would allow all the f—ed-up shit to happen to children, to allow such cruelty and undeserved suffering in this world, I didn't want anything to do with it. The last thing I expected while sitting in County was to have everything I thought about God shattered. The last time I was in jail, there was no one left to call, no one left to trick into rescuing me. I was looking at hard time, and I was all alone. Burning bridges has always been my specialty.

One day, about a month in, an older woman, another inmate, approached me and told me that she didn't think I belonged in there. She said she had a friend who would get me out, and all I needed to do was put some money on her books when I was free. She was heading to prison and had no reason to help, trust, or like me. And I had no reason to believe her. But that night, for the first time in years, I prayed. It was something like this: "I don't know who you are or if you're out there, and I know damn well I don't deserve it, but if you get me out of here, I'll do whatever you want me to do." Now I later learned that this was known as a foxhole prayer.

But something heard it and answered it, and I was bailed out of jail by some random old man who put his property up for my release. He wasn't a creep. He wasn't an asshole. He drove me to a little fast-food restaurant and waited five hours with me until I got someone to pick me up. He told me about his kids and his life and told me to make something of mine. I didn't have the wherewithal to realize what was happening, but after one more night of drunken chaos, another near arrest, and a call to a brother I hadn't spoken to in years, my life would never be the same.

On July 31, 2016, I was twelve-stepped, though I didn't know that was what was happening at the time. My brother's girlfriend, whom I had never met, brought me to her house, took me to my first AA meeting, let me stay with her for a few days, found me somewhere to go, and told me about the twelve steps of Alcoholics Anonymous. She spoke to my court-appointed attorney, found out that I was mandated to treatment, and got me into a sober living and an intensive outpatient therapy program. I was completely out of my comfort zone, had no idea what recovery was or how it worked, but I was either going to get sober or go to prison, and I'd die before I went to prison.

My first year sober was a roller coaster; I had left my old life behind entirely. I owned two T-shirts, one pair of sweatpants, and a pair of slides when I walked into sober living, and my recreation began. I got into a lot of trouble dating other women in my program, did a lot of silly things, and made a lot of memories while in treatment. I went to an outpatient therapy program, and though the thought was not mine, it was very clear that I had to face my trauma, face my past, or continue suffering, running, and ultimately die behind it.

I was not sure that I wanted to be sober, but I was sure that this was my only choice, and I gave it everything I had. I worked the twelve steps with a sponsor, had a hell of a spiritual experience, and was hungry to help others experience the miracle that I had. I went to court the day after my nine months sober. I watched as a judge read off my charges, read the details of my cases, and threw the papers off the stand and asked why he should even consider letting me go free. There were ten people in the gallery who showed up for me—mostly from my treatment team, my best friend from childhood, and my aunt. This army showing up for me when I never believed I deserved it and, most importantly, this power that I had come to experience as God showing up for me allowed me to walk out of that courtroom a free woman.

Ever since I surrendered to the process of sobriety, ever since I was taken in and *walked through this journey* by people who swore they understood, my life has slowly gotten better. I have experienced joy, freedom, peace, happiness, solidarity, and community that could never have been achieved with any drug. Sobriety has been a gift, though it does not mean my life is absent of pain, heartache, loss, depression, and loneliness, I have learned to *navigate* all these things with some semblance of grace, and I always come out on the other side more whole than before.

I have had to battle many different demons other than just drugs and alcohol. I continue to participate in trauma therapy, I take medications for my mental health, and I seek guidance when I come up against the various hardships in life. One of my biggest issues was always women: sick, codependent relationships that I sought out in order to "save" others when I couldn't even save myself. Today, as a result of the work that I put in to become whole by myself, I have found my soulmate, who inspires me, impresses me, and pushes me to be better every day. I know what it means to be loved and to love another. I have friends and relationships with people who matter, and the belief that this world only hosts darkness and unsafe people has been shattered. I never have to be alone again.

The most important gift that has been bestowed on me as a result of my sobriety and journey is the ability to truly affect others' lives. I was going to be a lawyer, so I thought. Instead, I have been called to help people—broken, hopeless, lonely people like myself. I thought I would always feel bitter, ashamed, guilty, dirty, and alone. Instead, all the pain in my life, the hearts I have broken and those who have broken mine, the trauma and guilt, the crime and desperation, every mistake and every harm I have caused or has been caused to me have purpose.

I know in my heart of hearts that I was not brought out of the darkness to live a simple, quiet life. I was brought out so that I can show others how to get out, as well; I have been given gifts that I use to help others heal and find purpose and meaning the same way I was allowed to. I have a love and passion for others that I could never have tapped into before. My career and my program are built around a calling to lead others from the darkness into a light they never knew existed. Every heart that I touch allows me to experience God in a way that I never knew was possible. The little girl who mistrusted everyone and everything has been set free; I am grateful to have lived so many lives and to have experienced the freedom and serenity that I never knew was possible.

Susan's Story

Never Too Old

I was in my mid sixties when my drinking became a real problem. I was probably in denial until I was about seventy years old. It was about that time that I first went to AA. I thought, before, I was functioning normally because I was still able to go about my daily routine, with (I thought) very little difficulty.

Growing up there was no alcohol abuse in my family or any of the families of my friends that I know of. There was always wine for ceremonial purposes, and even as a child, I always had a sip on Friday nights. I also remember not liking it that much. My dad usually had a beer with dinner, but that was all. Neither my parents nor my family drank much, nor did any of their friends or family. There was always alcohol in the house, but it never occurred to me to drink.

Fast-forward to high school. None of my friends drank, and neither did I. I smoked cigarettes at the age of fifteen, but that was the worst thing I did. Moving onto college, I married for a brief time. Again, I only drank socially. After my marriage dissolved, my girlfriends and I went bar hopping on Friday nights, but I never drank so much that I wasn't in control. I may have been high at times, but I never passed out, so to speak. But I did have hangovers the next day.

After five years of being single, I married again. I only drank socially. I do remember one time I went over to a friend's house and got really drunk to the point where her husband had to drive me home. Boy, was I sick! I swore I would never do that again, and I didn't.

The following years I was busy, working, raising my children, car-pooling, and so on, but I never thought to drink, except socially. Our friends didn't drink but socially. So alcohol wasn't an issue; besides, I didn't have time to drink.

It wasn't until my children were grown, married, and had children of their own that I started drinking more and more. First it was a drink when I was preparing dinner; then it was a drink after dinner. Soon it became, "Well, it's five o'clock somewhere," and there was drinking in the middle of the afternoon. I guess I knew I had a problem, but I thought I could control it. It was after I attended my nephew's wedding that I decided to get some help and went to AA. I attended several meet-ings; listened to numerous horror stories; and thought, "I am not really on the same page as these other people. I just need to learn to control my drinking." But I got a sponsor and started following the steps. After ninety days free of alcohol, I guessed I was cured. One little drink once in a while wouldn't hurt me. Boy, was I wrong!

My husband has been an incredible help and extremely supportive throughout my journey. He doesn't drink at all because of some medical conditions. He always has been there for me. My nonalcoholic friends have been wonderful and have been supportive all the way. The same with my children. When I finally told them of my problem and what I was doing about it, they were extremely relieved and said they were reaching the point where they were about to tell me I couldn't see my wonderful, beautiful, brilliant grandchildren if I did not stop drinking. If that isn't incentive, I don't know what is. Both children and their spouses have been so supportive, and I am truly blessed to have so much support from everyone.

I was sober five years on April 19, 2021, and I am truly grateful for every day. I am now a seventy-seven-year-old alcohol-free individual, but I am still a recovering alcoholic, and I am one drink away from being a drunk. One day at a time, even with COVID-19, I still have Zoom meetings, and I cherish the friendships that I have made and the knowledge that I have gained.

So that's my story, and my journey continues. I can't say I'm grateful I am an alcoholic, but I can say that I never want to go back to drinking. And I am grateful that there are all these tools to help me on my journey.

Chapter Seven

Making Restitution

Steps 8 and 9

STEP 8: "MADE A LIST OF ALL PERSONS WE HAD HARMED AND BECAME WILLING TO MAKE AMENDS TO THEM ALL."[1]

Having completed some crucial steps on the heroic journey of deciding to be better people and of asking God, in whatever way we chose to do so, to make us the best we can be, more work needs to be accomplished. Once again, the heroes are reminded that they cannot just quit drinking and forever be nice. Continuing effort is required. It is time to repair some of the damage that has been done to other people and relationships in their lives.

The heroes have already made a list of all such people when they took the fourth step. It is now time to review this list and see who needs to be added or to see what additional harms have been recalled that were done to people already on the list. No thought should be given to the actual amends making at this time because this may cause the heroes to lose courage and leave someone or something off the list. They must keep their eyes on the road directly in front of them.

Once again on the journey, the heroes are called on to be willing. This is not the first time in the quest for salvation and recovery that willingness is demanded of the heroes. In the first step, the heroes must be willing to admit defeat. In the second step, the heroes are asked to be willing to believe in a power greater than themselves. The third step requires the willingness to surrender one's life and will to the care of that higher power. Step 4 requires the willingness to make an honest and thorough self-appraisal, and step 5 requires the willingness to confess their shortcomings in life to another person and to a higher power. Step 6 calls for the willingness to release those qualities that have sullied their souls and behaviors, and in taking step 7, the heroes must be willing to ask God to remove their defects of character.

Now, in confronting the eighth step, the refusal of the call to adventure rears its ugly dragon head once more. Reluctance is encountered time and time again along the way and must be overcome. It is worth remembering on this heroic journey that a promise of help has been made, spiritual help. As O. Hobart Mowrer says, "You alone can do it, but you can't do it alone."[2] The hero going it alone on the journey will most certainly get lost in the wilderness (and get very thirsty).

Several fears may strike the hero at this juncture of the journey. Fear of embarrassment, shame, financial compromise or ruin, loss of important relationships, loss of job, the reopening of old wounds, and even imprisonment may be consequences of the revelation of certain facts to others. Courage is called for. Paul Tillich in *The Courage to Be* talks of the three types of anxiety or fear that threaten us: "that of fate and death, that of emptiness and loss of meaning, and that of guilt and condemnation."[3] He says that such anxiety is inherent in human existence. As long as we live, we cannot be entirely separated from fear.

Finding courage does not involve proceeding in the absence of fear. Courage involves the willingness to act in the presence of fear. Where does the hero find such courage? As noted, the heroes have been promised help, and in this regard, they can benefit from a mentor, the sponsor who has been a guide along the way and who assures them that this step has been accomplished by the sponsors themselves, and they survived it nicely. Moreover, by now, they have learned that countless others have taken this step to their own benefit. Once again, the focus on the eighth step is not on the actual making of amends but rather only on finding the willingness to do so. It does not have to be made harder than it really is. The heroes know what is next, but by focusing on the actual step, they can control their anxiety about step 9.

Another issue representing a challenge on this leg of the heroic journey is that of forgiveness. There are three aspects to consider: obtaining forgiveness from others, forgiving others (including God), and forgiving oneself. Interpersonal difficulties are at the heart of most problems in life. Often the person owed the amends has been the subject of a long-held and treasured resentment. Heroes may feel more like victims of a hurt than the cause of a hurt to another. Once again, the guidance of a sponsor will help focus the attention on the hero's side of the street. Neither what the other party may have done to them nor how the other party may respond to their making of amends can be allowed to have anything to do with the course of their journeys. They are events along the way but will only cause trouble if the heroes let themselves get sidetracked from the job at hand.

As to the expectation of being forgiven or even being treated graciously by the person the hero is making amends to, this should not even be a consideration. However, there is value in asking for forgiveness while not expecting it. One value lies in the potential benefit to the other person. By asking for forgiveness, the hero may give the other person an unexpected opportunity to release a long-held resentment and lighten a burden. As a practical matter, the responses will range widely from total forgiveness to outright hostility or possibly a refusal to talk. Expecting either an apology or acceptance of the amends from the person is a good way of developing a whole new resentment when the expectation is not met. Frequently, amends making does lead to an improvement in the relationship, and while this is a desirable outcome, it does not determine or control the success of taking of the step.

Still, preparation at this juncture must include thinking through how the heroes will handle potential rejection of their apologies. And of course, often it must be more than an apology. There may be money to repay or other situations to make right. Emotions are likely to surface and must be handled in a mature and controlled manner. If the journeyer feels unprepared to face a certain individual, then the actual amends making needs to be postponed. Again, at this stage, all that is required is the willingness to proceed. Ultimately, this segment of the heroic journey more than anything else is a quest for healing. Dag Hammarskjöld writes about the importance of the attempt to repair broken relationships:

> Forgiveness is the answer to the child's dream of a miracle by which what is broken is made whole again, what is soiled is again made clean. The dream explains why we need to be forgiven, and why we must forgive. In the presence of God, nothing stands between Him and us—we *are* forgiven. But we *cannot* feel His presence if anything is allowed to stand between ourselves and others.[4]

The typical addict is a guilt-ridden individual, filled with self-recrimination and regret.

Self-forgiveness, while not explicitly stated as a step in the process, nevertheless does occur as the result of the steps. Dr. Jerry Hirschfield says, "It is as important to forgive ourselves as it is the other person. If we do not forgive ourselves, we cannot forgive others. . . . Our willingness to make amends must stem from a true desire to forgive and forget the other person's wrong as well as ours."[5] As Bill Wilson says at the end of his chapter on the eighth step in *Twelve Steps and Twelve Traditions*, "Whenever our pencil falters, we can fortify and cheer ourselves by remembering what AA experience in this Step has meant to others. It is the beginning of the end of isolation from our fellows and from God."[6]

Let us consider the story of Jacob in the context of the eighth step. As told earlier, he had cheated his brother Esau out of his father's blessing and had also extracted his birthright from him for a bowl of soup. Fleeing for his life, he had gone to Harran, far to the East, where he stayed with his uncle Laban. While there, he acquired two wives, two concubines, children, servants, and much livestock. Near the end of his stay with Laban, he tricked Laban and took much of his flocks of animals.

On the run from Laban, he headed back to Canaan, where he had to face the music with his brother Esau. The day before the expected meeting, he got word that Esau was coming to meet him with an army of four hundred men. What to do? Esau was certainly at the top of Jacob's amends list. (When confronted with a decision about with whom to start making amends, much needs to be considered, and every case is different. One approach is to do the hardest and the easiest amends first. Jacob was at the point of facing up to his most difficult amends.)

He made preparations. He brought his entourage across the river and then crossed back to spend the night alone. He prayed to God with some humility, but he also reminded God of God's promises to him. In the night, he wrestled with a being described as a man but who had characteristics that suggested that he was divine. There is more than one way to interpret this event. He seemed to be struggling with himself—his fears, as well as with his inner god—and his emotions and his soul were both involved.

He was praying for and struggling for the courage and the willingness to take the next step, symbolized by the crossing of the River Jabbok. At daybreak, Jacob received a blessing from the stranger. The blessing included a change of his name from Jacob to Israel, symbolic of the spiritual growth achieved through the struggle. He had completed the eighth step of his heroic journey, and it was time to cross the river.

STEP 9: "MADE DIRECT AMENDS TO SUCH PEOPLE WHEREVER POSSIBLE, EXCEPT WHEN TO DO SO WOULD INJURE THEM OR OTHERS."[7]

From the very start of the journey, the heroes make indirect amends simply by living sober and changing their behavior. Hopefully, this will be noticed and appreciated by friends and family along the way. Time since the last drink has elapsed, during which the heroes have been encouraged by improvement in their outlook and quality of life. These benefits, along with the hard work done thus far, have prepared our heroes for what may be the most intimidating step of all—directly facing those they have harmed with the truth about themselves, specifically the actual harms done, some of which those harmed may not have even suspected.

Once again, courage is called for, as well as the faith that this step is necessary and will be for the best. Now, for the first time on the journey, judgments will have to be made about exactly what actions to take. Having come this far, many people will still be burdened by self-serving motives and lack awareness of the extent to which their current behavior may continue to be potentially harmful to others, especially those they love and who love them. Are there people who should not be approached just yet? Are there issues that should be left unspoken about for fear of harming innocent persons? If an amends could result in loss of job or incarceration, then the heroes must consult with those who would suffer as a result and be willing to postpone an amends or possibly let it go indefinitely. The heroes do not have the right to attempt to expiate their guilt at the expense of others. Nor should the heroes make such important decisions without the counsel of a trusted advisor. If an amends is postponed, then it should be after wise counsel and consideration. Remember, the heroes are now required to live on a spiritual basis if they expect to be reborn to a new life.

In the Big Book, there is a section that talks about in what condition of spirit the hero will find themselves after completing the ninth step.[8] This material is frequently read at AA meetings, referred to as the Promises or the Ninth Step Promises. They are introduced by the statement "If we have been painstaking about this phase of our development, we will be amazed before we are halfway through."[9] Note that Bill does not say if we have been casual or lackadaisical or superficial or insincere about this phase. Thoroughness and fearlessness have been required at every step. Let there be no mistake: Taking a heroic journey calls for heroism.

So let us look at where our heroes might expect to be at this stage. The first promise is "We are going to know a new freedom and a new happiness."[10] What is significant about this statement is the use of the word *new*. Our heroes may have experienced a sense of freedom in the past. Indeed, they may have grossly abused the freedoms they were privileged to have. Most people can look back on times when they may have been happy. But the promise is for a freedom and happiness *never before experienced—new*.

Earlier in the Big Book, Bill Wilson uses the phrase *the bondage of self*.[11] Paradoxically, as the heroes dig deeper and deeper into their examination of self, they are increasingly free from the chains that tied them to their narcissistic cores. They are no longer studying themselves because they find themselves to be so fascinating or so marvelous and important. Nor are they as self-preoccupied because of fear or insecurity. Now they look into the mirror and deeper to find the characteristics that keep them enslaved. The more self-centered people are, the more they are bound in a self-induced and self-enforced prison.

Happiness is best achieved by right living rather than by direct pursuit thereof. For example, it is a spiritual axiom that the happiness involved in giving far exceeds the happiness of receiving. The statement "It is more blessed to give than to receive" is one of the best-known biblical quotations.[12] It has been the experience of the people in the fellowship of AA that the greatest of satisfactions is drawn from helping others. Indeed, helping others is a core principle of AA and is believed to be necessary for ongoing recovery. I look at this in greater depth in step 12.

The next promise is "We will not regret the past nor wish to shut the door on it."[13] This is a hard one. Heroes can come to accept all the suffering they have experienced as what was necessary to get them to where they are today. Indeed, they, in their new state of happiness, can recognize that the only way they could be where they are is because they have come from where they had been. It is harder to accept having hurt others, especially loved ones and most especially their children, to the point of no longer having any regrets.

The journey we were on before recovery was filled with potholes and other obstacles, mostly of our own making, that we managed poorly. Some of this we just must live with. As a practical matter, I do not believe the past ever looks like a Garden of Eden, but on the heroic quest, one learns how to live with the past, to accept forgiveness, and to forgive oneself. This is one of those places that helps one understand that this is a lifetime journey. Our heroes will periodically recall some incident or circumstance that arouses a thought of regret and feelings of guilt, shame, and embarrassment. This is an occurrence that Bill Wilson refers to as "morbid reflection."[14] Having come this far on his journey, though, they will have the capacity to forgive themselves once again, to let it go, and to be grateful for their lives as they are today. The more progress one has made with ego deflation, the less vulnerable one is to recurrent pangs of shame.

The next promise is "We will comprehend the word *serenity* and we will know peace."[15] Indeed, *serenity* describes a state of peacefulness. Having lived the life of active addiction, experiencing some peacefulness is a blessing indeed. One of the most respected writers in the recovery field says, "Serenity or peace of mind is not a goal in itself. It is the result of a revolution in our thinking; a revolution, in our case, brought about by our efforts to apply the Twelve Steps of the AA program to our daily life."[16]

Emmet Fox, a writer whose work had a great influence on the thinking of the early AA members, says, "Serenity itself is only to be had by prayer, and by the forgiving of others, and of oneself. But serenity you must have, before you can make any true spiritual progress; and it is serenity, that fundamental tranquility of soul, that Jesus refers to by the word 'peace'—the peace that passes all human understanding."[17] Such an untroubled state of mind is clearly a gift that comes about through trusting a higher power and thinking about and living life differently.

The next promise says "No matter how far down the scale we have gone, we will see how our experience can benefit others." The following promise complements this one: "That feeling of uselessness and self-pity will disappear."[18] One of the great causes of pain and anxiety in life is the thought that one's life has no meaning or purpose. Man

cannot have a life like an animal that walks on four legs and just *be*.
For people, their being must ultimately *mean* something, or their lives
become intolerable. For most people, the discovery that a major purpose of life is to be of service to others, to improve the world in some
small way, not only shines a light on the road ahead, but also, looking
backward, one can see how experience has prepared one for such service. Bill Wilson repeatedly emphasizes the importance of being useful,
stressing how one's experience has prepared the recovering alcoholic to
help others who are still at the beginning of their quest for a new life.

The promise of the disappearance of self-pity is profound in at least
two respects. First, addicts must face up to the fact that, in some way,
they have believed the false and miserable "poor-me story" that they
have been telling themselves. The story is nurtured for weeks, months,
and years and believed to be true by the storyteller, if not by anyone else.

A friend recalls actually thinking that he was the world's unhappiest
person. He estimates that the world population at that time was at least
four billion people. How likely was it that he was the unhappiest of
four billion people, especially given that he slept indoors, had shoes to
wear, and had at least something to eat every day? This illustrates the
remarkable distortion in thinking that the addict or person affected by
another's addiction can have.

There is an interesting fact about self-pity: It is a close relative of
resentment. It is a fact that, if such people would make a list of all the
reasons they felt sorry for themselves and another list of all their resentments, they would discover that it is the same list. The second reason I
believe the promise is profound is that it says that self-pity *slips away*.
No specific or direct action must be taken to attack self-pity itself. By
working the first nine steps, the heroes have profoundly changed and
have acquired *gratitude*, a direct antidote to the poison of self-pity. It
is a fact that it is impossible to experience both self-pity and gratitude
in the same moment. Self-pity is defeated by the heroic journey itself.

The next promise reads, "Our whole attitude and outlook on life will
change."[19] Have you ever heard "Life is a bitch, and then you die?"
Well, I have, many, many times. Suffering can engender bad attitudes,
as well as spiritual transformation. In fact, for recovering people on a
heroic quest, in most cases both occur—first the bad attitude and then
the transformation. So, my response to the "Life is a bitch" is "No, but

it is a struggle." It is only a "bitch" when people try to deal with the struggle on their own.

People become deeply cynical, sometimes with justification based on their experiences. One can have a bad attitude for many reasons. When I talk to people, I tell them it is their attitude, and only they can change it—and they can change it if they want to. As they progress on their journey, going from despair to a glimmering of hope to having more positive experiences and success, the hope grows exponentially until it is a new outlook on life—if they have been thorough and taken great pains to walk the walk of the steps.

The next promise is "Fear of people and of economic insecurity will leave us."[20] Note, this is really two separate promises, and once again, these conditions just *leave*. Fear of people is an inherent human characteristic. It derives initially from being born in a state of helplessness and of a growing awareness of one's helplessness. Everyone in childhood has the experience of being hurt by other people. One's increasing sense of self is intimately connected to an awareness of one's helplessness and vulnerability.

Human development takes many years of maturation. The acquisition of the skills and confidence needed to make friends, provide for one's own needs, establish goals, and ultimately achieve mature psychosexual relationships are some of the most significant of life tasks that we all as humans are challenged with. During the process of this development, many things can occur to slow or disrupt the natural development so that fully functioning emotional adulthood is not achieved. Not the least of these disruptions is abuse of drugs and alcohol during adolescence and early adulthood. Other causes of such failure of development can and do fill textbooks. Nowhere will this deficiency in ego development be more obvious than in one's relationships with others.

If there is one personality characteristic that is universally present in addicts, it is low self-esteem. People with low self-esteem are going to fear people because, in their interactions with others, they are certain that their glaring inadequacy as people will be exposed. Such exposure, they fear, will lead to rejection and even abandonment, ultimately leading to further loneliness, feelings of failure, and self-hate. Fear of abandonment, in my view, is the single most compelling and universal of all human fears. And drinking can only cover all this up for so long.

Yet in this chapter of the Big Book, we are told that fear of people will leave us.

If it does (and most people who have reached this stage of their heroic journey will attest that it does), then what has changed? Presumably, the rest of the world is about as it was before the journey commenced. Therefore, the heroes have changed and remarkably so. Our heroes have stopped the addictive spiral, trusted a higher power, looked deeply within themselves, admitted their faults, resolved to be better people, asked for help in this regard from their higher power, became willing to set things right with those they have harmed, and made such amends wherever possible. And now, amazingly, the self-hate, the insecurity, and the fear of others is markedly diminished, if not gone altogether. While this is remarkable, and while it is true, the only catch is that it will only remain so if our heroes continue on their quest.

Fear of economic insecurity is the other promise included in this sentence. Notice that the promise is not that economic insecurity will leave but only that the *fear* of economic insecurity will leave. In the world in which we live, our basic needs are all dependent on having the capital resources to provide for them. This is just a fact of life. I have known people who had millions of dollars in assets and little to no debt, and they still worried about their financial security. At some point, one has to trust that one's needs will be met. The trust that our heroes have gained in their higher power through their journeys thus far is considerable. The travelers have acquired the sense that they will not be let down, that whatever situation may arise, they will be able to manage it. There is no easy answer to this. Sometimes life is a struggle.

This leads us directly into the next promise: "We will intuitively know how to handle situations which used to baffle us."[21] In the prior lives of addicts, just as in anyone's life, situations periodically arose in which a decision was called for. Typically, at those times, addicts were either torn by indecision and worry or either impulsively rushed in and said or did something—anything—without giving it two seconds of thought. People who have traveled from being unable to handle life in a rational, thoughtful way to being able to *intuitively* manage life are truly remarkable. They have done a great deal more than quit drinking. They have been *transformed*. They have gone from being in a chronic state of confusion, despair, and inability to get through their day in a healthful, self-respecting, and reasonable manner to displaying wisdom and good judgment and earning the respect of themselves and others.

Rev. Howard Thurman writes, "The ability to know what is the right thing to do in a given circumstance is a sheer gift from God."[22] Indeed, for most heroes, this realization comes as a sudden revelation at a time in which they are in a situation where they realize they would have previously been at a loss for what to say or do; yet now, they unaccountably are able to say or do just the right thing or have the presence of mind to say or do nothing. At such a time we hear people saying, "That wasn't me who just did that. The person that I used to be would have managed that situation very badly. I cannot believe how much I have changed."

This segues into the final Ninth Step Promise, which is "We will suddenly realize that God is doing for us what we could not do for ourselves."[23] The heroes are flooded with a sense of gratitude and newborn confidence that the road they are traveling is indeed transforming their lives. And they are certain beyond any doubt that such a transformation could only have been brought about by their higher power.

Taking the first nine steps brings the heroes to a point of completion of what is probably the most transformative part of their journeys. They are not drinking, drugging, gambling, or engaging in whatever other addictively compulsive behavior they had been in the grip of. They have placed their faith in a higher power, completed a rigorous self-examination, promised themselves to be a better person, remained in the care of their higher power for this purpose, and rectified the conflicts and debts they owed to others insofar as was possible up to this point.

This concludes this stage of the adventure. The dragon has been slain. Now it is time for the return to the world of their origins, to bring home the treasure that they have obtained on their journeys thus far. There is not a clear demarcation point, for certainly their ventures into amends making, both direct and indirect, have already significantly repaired their world. But here they enter a new phase—that of consolidating their gains, making their world better each day, venturing further on the road of self-knowledge, deepening their relationship with their higher power, and making certain that the dragon doesn't put its head back on its shoulders and eat them alive.

Now, let us return to Jacob, who just completed his eighth step and crossed the river, symbolic of the growth and transformation that occurred within him. He stepped on the opposite shore a new person. He was about to make an amends of Herculean proportions, hoping that Esau wouldn't kill him in retaliation for stealing their father Isaac's blessing. He sent ahead of him wave after wave of gifts: two hundred female goats, twenty male goats; thirty female camels with their young; forty cows and ten bulls; and twenty female and ten male donkeys. Accompanying each wave of gifts were servants who were instructed to tell Esau that these were gifts from Jacob, who was coming up behind them.

When they came in sight of each other, Jacob sent the women and children ahead of him, and then he approached Esau, bowing seven times to the ground. It worked out. They hugged, kissed, and made up, after a fashion. I don't think they met again until they buried their father. The point here is that Jacob knew he had to make the amends, prayed about it, and struggled to find the courage and willingness, and when the day arrived, he went straight ahead and did it.

This is the model to follow in making a difficult amends. It is also the amends he made first. He certainly still owed an amends to his father and in fact was very slow to proceed with it. He still had some character building to do. This also will be the case for most people on their heroic twelve step journey. Heroes must move ahead, and even though, they may not have completed all their amends, presumably for reasons of distance, convenience, or sound judgment, it is time to move on to step 10. But first, let's hear from Steve.

Steve's Story

Seeking God

I was brought up in a conservative Jewish home, went to Hebrew school for many years, attended temple regularly (at least for the holidays), and was bar mitzvahed. However, over time, as I went to college and studied philosophy, I began to question religion and the idea of God. I had struggled, like many, with why bad things happened in the world if there was a God, and my attitude toward God became defiant. I was very affected around that time by a Randy Newman song with the lines "I tear down your temples, how blind you all must be. I take from you your children and you say 'How blessed are we!' You all must be crazy to put your faith in me. That's why I love mankind. You really need me. That's why I love mankind." The idea that others shared my trepidation regarding God and religion was enlightening.

I had also gravitated toward a scientific view of the world with strong belief in the scientific method and the idea that, if it couldn't be proved scientifically and wasn't subject to laws of cause and effect, it wasn't real. So I began to identify as an atheist. This was helped by the fact that my mother, while she had ensured I went to Hebrew school and had a bar mitzvah, was not religious, although both my mother and father were involved in the temple. I also think I became more cynical overall when my parents divorced as I began high school.

My first experience with drinking alcoholically was at a Passover seder at my nana's house when I was, maybe six or seven. I remember quickly downing each of the four ceremonial glasses of Mogen David wine that burned going down like whiskey and eagerly awaiting the next. Later, when I was a freshman in high school, I got very drunk (beer) at the celebration of my grandfather's wedding (after my nana passed away), and when I got home, I was terribly sick.

I was always kind of a socially isolated, awkward, bookish, good kid and was very resistant to some of the experimentation with smoking and drinking that kids my age participated in. But in my senior year in high school, I wound up with a bunch of guys going to a dance at the Statler Hilton Hotel in Boston. We had gotten some wine, and I spent most of the night on the floor of a men's room stall, throwing up. (I can still taste the Boones Farm coming up if I think about it.) But the following Monday, in school, a lot of the guys were very chummy with me, recalling what a great time we had had, and I had discovered how I fit into the in crowd, and alcohol became very central to my social life and who I was.

I also had found, around this time, an effective social tool in humor, specifically sarcasm, and discovered I had an ear for it and a good repartee. This had been honed around my family as a useful tool to reduce tension around fighting and my mother's rage. When my parents got divorced, I also began using it to act out in school with a lot of classroom wisecracking, and my grades began to suffer at the same time. The divorce precipitated a lot of financial challenges and conflict, which became the foundation for my fears of financial insecurity and being, as Jackson Brown says, "caught between the longing for love and the struggle for the legal tender."

By the time I started attending college and had no real restrictions on my drinking, I had become, pretty much, a daily drinker, supplemented a little with some drugs on the side. But by the time I graduated college, I was a pure alcoholic. I had also started smoking cigarettes because, between high school and college, I had started dating the girl who would later become my first wife, and she wanted us to try pot. But I had been told by someone I wouldn't get anything out of that if I had never smoked a cigarette, so I tried smoking and was instantly a chain smoker for the next nineteen years.

When my marriage began to erode, largely due to my alcoholism and workaholism, I began attending AA meetings, mostly because I wanted to quit smoking, but every time I quit, I'd have a couple of drinks and would start smoking again. So I started going to AA initially to help me quit smoking, thinking AA would teach me how to not drink long enough to quit smoking. Once there, I realized pretty quickly that I fit the description of an alcoholic. (I actually didn't quit smoking until I had been sober for about three and a half years.)

I almost left my first AA meeting because the steps on the wall mentioned God, and there was a speaker talking about her personal relationship with God. I also didn't identify with a lot of the stories because I was fortunate enough to have come in before I had lost much; I'd never been arrested, had a DUI, been in a fight, or lost a job, and my marriage was still (marginally) intact; other common indicators were absent.

Fortunately, I was told those things hadn't happened *yet*, and if I kept drinking, they would, so I should identify and not compare. I was terrified of losing my job, so I kept coming. Another inducement to continue with AA attendance was the social aspect, because I had become pretty socially isolated, and I enjoyed the company of people at AA.

I read the AA Big Book. In addition to learning about alcoholism being a combination of a physical allergy and a mental compulsion, I read a line that says, "Are you now or would you ever be willing to believe that there is a power greater than yourself?" That seemed like a pretty broad requirement, to which I could not imagine saying, "No, I will *never* believe there is any power greater than myself." I also heard in what's known as "How It Works" (that's read at the beginning of many meetings), that "no human power could have relieved our alcoholism, but God could and would if he were *sought*," and it was pointed out that I didn't need to find God. I could stay sober if I just *sought* a power greater than myself. I just needed to *seek* him. And I've been seeking him ever since. The language of "God as we understood him" in AA was very crucial to my getting sober, as was the third tradition, that the only requirement for membership is a desire to stop drinking. Had it required embracing a specific religious or spiritual view, I don't think it would have stuck.

Seeking God included a renewed interest in Judaism, going to things like a dharma study group, some meditating, tai chi, and a lot of reading. In addition to the Big Book and *Twelve and Twelve* of AA, one book that was very pivotal for me during this time was *The Tao of Physics* by Fritjof Capra, which helped me reconcile my scientific point of view with the concept of spirituality. I was also affected by *When Bad Things Happen to Good People* by Rabbi Harold Kushner, which helped me resolve somewhat the problem of evil. (Basically, if God created a world with free will, then evil stems from *that*, and God sometimes cries, too, as the result rather than being the cause.) I was also affected a lot by Scott Peck's *The Road Less Traveled* and *Finding God* by Sonsino and Syme.

It was around this time I was advised in AA to "fake it until you make it" and "act as if," so I got in the habit, as advised, of getting on my knees every morning and praying and meditating, which I began doing and have been doing ever since. (Getting on my knees was new because it was not part of the Jewish prayer tradition.) My ritual includes a few miscellaneous prayers that have changed over time, but my view of this is not that it's what I call a walkie-talkie to God but that praying affects *me*—not God. A lot of this today is asking for help removing my character defects: "Please remove my character defects so that I may better serve thy will. Thank you for keeping me away from a drink and a cigarette yesterday and all the days before. I pray you'll keep me away from a drink and a cigarette, overeating, sarcasm, covetousness, envy, fear of financial insecurity, and sexualizing women today and all the days to come."

(So far, the only ones I've prevailed over are drinking and cigarettes. Most of my other defects have seen incremental improvement but have been far from removed. But I continue to "trudge the road of happy destiny" with the goal of improving my character. Before I end, I usually say, "I arise, O God, to do thy will," which admittedly is a little odd for a self-proclaimed atheist.)

I struggle a lot with the language in AA literature that says, "Nothing happens in God's world without a reason." I was never able to accept that because I do believe in free will, although I was eventually able to believe that, as I always say, one thing follows another and that the world is unfolding as it should. And the less I try and "push the river," the better things go for me and everybody else. Today, I would say that, while I believe in a power greater than myself and believe in the power of prayer, meditation, and intuitive thought, I no longer have the need to understand the *mechanism*, no more than I need to understand how an internal combustion engine works to rely on a car. And I have stopped trying to understand it or figure it out.

I used to say I was an alcoholic because I was an atheist ("Life has no point, so we might as well eat, drink, and be merry"), but I later came to believe that I first became an atheist because I'm an alcoholic, and at some point, the idea of having beliefs and principles conflicted with my desire to drink. Throughout my thirty-four years in AA, as I have struggled with my relationship with a power greater than myself, I have wound up in a place where I generally identify as an atheist, in that I don't believe in the idea of a traditional Judeo-Christian big-white-guy-with-a-beard-in-the sky concept of God. However, I believe there are dimensions beyond what we can perceive that we will never and cannot ever fully understand.

But the idea of a power greater than myself is still useful and plays a role in my life, particularly in helping me work the twelve steps of AA; stay sober; and continually improve my character, which I now accept as an end in itself. I rely on that power, whatever it is and which may be internal or in the ether, to help me identify my character defects and improve the person that I am, as well as provide helpful, intuitive thought. In fact, I have come to accept and believe the idea, as discussed in AA, that, when troubled or disturbed, I pause and wait for an intuitive thought, and the answers will come, and that will become a working part of the mind. That has been my experience and is another phenomenon of which I no longer need to understand the mechanism.

Finally, an essential part of my quest for sobriety includes service, which, for me, mostly takes the form of service in AA. This includes working with newcomers, participating in a home group, sponsoring people, speaking when asked, being present and participating in meetings, and being available any time there is another alcoholic who needs help. The foundation of the AA program is that one alcoholic helps another and that service helps the first stay sober. I actively seek relationships with newcomers, and when someone calls me, I always thank them for calling me (because talking to the newcomer helps keep me sober).

Along the way, I have also sought help with therapy, as well as CODA, Al-Anon, and some other twelve step programs, but ultimately, I found myself working "forty-eight or sixty steps" and being on the verge of a drink. So years ago, I stopped the other programs and since have focused on working a good AA program and addressing my other character defects through the sixth and seventh and tenth steps.

When I found AA and the twelve steps, not only was I struggling with alcoholism, but also as a result, my emotional, physical, and spiritual pilot lights had pretty much gone out. Today, far beyond what my expectation might have been thirty-four years ago (I don't believe I would have made it much past age forty—I am now pushing seventy), my quest is to stay and die sober and become the best person I can be in the meantime.

Chapter Eight

Returning to the Kingdom with the Treasure

Steps 10, 11, and 12

STEP 10: "CONTINUED TO TAKE PERSONAL INVENTORY, AND WHEN WE WERE WRONG, PROMPTLY ADMITTED IT."[1]

The last three of the twelve steps describe an ongoing journey. One way of thinking about this is to say that this is the maintenance phase, a time when, each day, the gains made are reinforced and strengthened. It is important to recognize that these three steps are to be done daily. The structure of the twelve steps is such that the first three and the last three steps are to be taken every day.

Every morning on this ongoing heroic journey, heroes must remember that their addiction is a chronic illness; it has not disappeared. Next, it is necessary to remember that one's higher power can keep one sober today. And then, they must make a decision and ask their higher power to take charge of their will and life for that day. These are the first three steps. Steps 4 through 9 are structured as the part of the adventure that brings the heroes to the point of spiritual renewal and contented sobriety. (For many on this journey, a repeat visit to steps 4 through 9 is an indispensable element in their recovery.)

Step 10 is the step of self-awareness. No longer can the heroes charge through life without conscious regard to how they are thinking, feeling, and acting. They now have done an inventory of their assets, as well as their shortcomings, and even though they have asked God to remove the shortcomings, there is no realistic chance that will happen, certainly not in its entirety. Even though transformed, the heroes are still human.

Bill Wilson discovered that, for himself, continued practice of self-awareness was crucial for his own survival. In *The Language of the Heart*, he states, "Long ago I was able to see that I'd have to keep up my self-analysis or else blow my top completely. Though driven by stark necessity, this continuous self-revelation—to myself and to others—was rough medicine to take. But years of repetition has made this job far easier."[2] It is important for the hero to realize that perfection is not the goal. Humanity is the goal. Thich Nhat Hanh writes, "The miracle is not to walk on water. The miracle is to walk on the green earth in the present moment."[3]

The emphasis must always be on the journeyer's own side of the street. Taking another's inventory is dangerous, unless it is coupled with the realization that the reason the other person evokes so much irritation and anger in us is that we see in them a reflection of our own shortcomings. We turn again to Thich Nhat Hanh: "There are many conflicting feelings and ideas within us, and it is important to look deeply and know what is going on. If we go back to ourselves and touch our feelings, we will see the ways that we furnish fuel for the wars going on inside."[4]

In the execution of the fourth step, our heroes have compiled an extensive list of their defects of character, their human failings. Hopefully, they have their list of their assets of character, as well. Some people are advised to burn their fourth step in a ceremony as a symbolic way of letting go of the past. It may be advisable to do this to destroy any evidence of past wrongdoing that could incriminate the hero in one way or another. However, I do think it would be important to retain the list of character assets and defects, for now it can be put to another good use: as a guide to the daily tenth step self-examination.

Many authors recommend making a list of personal characteristics to cultivate and others to eliminate. Jon Kabat-Zinn, who writes about stress management, especially for patients with chronic pain, has a list of characteristics that are positive and can reduce stress and one of negative traits that increase stress. On the positive side, he includes

optimism; the ability to let go of a bad event; the capacity to recognize that things can improve; the belief that one can effect some control of his/her life (through the exercise of good judgment); a sense of humor, being able to laugh at oneself; a strong sense of coherence, that life makes some sense, that life can be comprehensible and meaningful; a spirit of engagement in life; seeing problems as challenges; self-confidence; valuing other people and relationships; believing in goodness; ability to trust; compassion.[5]

These are characteristics that our heroes have been cultivating on their journey, some of which I spoke of as coming to fruition in the Ninth Step Promises.

On the negative side, leading to worsening of stress, Dr. Kabat-Zinn says are "hopelessness; helplessness; feeling out of control; cynicism; hostility towards others; feeling unable to face life's challenges; inability to express feelings; social isolation."[6] Neither list is comprehensive, but both are nevertheless useful. What is important is the willingness to look at oneself daily and honestly. As Stephanie Covington writes, "Admitting the truth to ourselves empowers us to live a spiritual life—to be fully who we are."[7] And Jerry Hirschfield has this to say about honesty in the Tenth Step: "The daily practice of the Tenth Step maintains our honesty, without which we cannot have humility, without which we cannot have the daily spiritual nourishment we need for ongoing development."[8] To that I might add, "and neither can we stay sober."

There are several approaches to the tenth step. Any or all of them can be part of each person's design for living. Many people have as part of their morning meditation, of which I say more in the next section, a review of the day ahead. Heroes can think about what situations they may likely experience at work, at home, or in other activities. They may think about what emotions may be aroused in those situations and how they may best prepare themselves. They will check themselves to see how they are feeling at that moment. They may identify one or two character defects that seem to be giving them the most trouble so that they can be mindful of them as they go through their day. As part of this exercise, they may pray for help in overcoming their obstacles to serenity.

Another approach to the tenth step is for the heroes to be more aware in each moment of how they are thinking, feeling, and behaving. Should they realize when an emotion is affecting them in a negative manner and remembering that they want to be relieved of these feelings, they can ask for help from their higher power. Likewise, they can note how they are speaking to others, how they are behaving, and what thoughts they are thinking. If a resentment crops up, then they can take note of this and release it. This approach takes practice, but if they stay with it, it can become ingrained as a daily recovery practice. This will give them time to think and to gain a better understanding of what their part is in whatever is troubling them.

Lastly, it is well to spend time in the evening reviewing the adventures of the day. Our heroes can recall what events took place, whom they encountered, how they related to others, what emotions were felt, what positive or negative thoughts entered their minds, and how they managed the negativity that arose within them. They can experience gratitude that they had a sober day and that they had all the help they needed to deal with whatever stressed them during the day. Indeed, many people write out a gratitude list every day as a way of keeping themselves in a positive space. Along with the gratitude list, any form of journaling one's thoughts and feelings is a useful exercise and provides material that can be referred back to so that one can see the progress being made.

STEP 11: "SOUGHT THROUGH PRAYER AND MEDITATION TO IMPROVE OUR CONSCIOUS CONTACT WITH GOD *AS WE UNDERSTOOD HIM,* PRAYING ONLY FOR KNOWLEDGE OF HIS WILL FOR US AND THE POWER TO CARRY THAT OUT."[9]

If the tenth step is the step of self-awareness, then the eleventh step is the step of God awareness. One aspect of self-awareness is the recognition that we can't take this journey alone, so step 11 is the logical sequel to step 10. Step 11 is another step that needs to be taken daily. Daily prayer is a common practice in most religions, as well as in the lives of countless other people who are not directly affiliated with a religion. Implicit in this practice is the belief on the part of the practitioner that life is best lived with God as a companion and helpmate.

Prayer can be either communal or done in solitude. It can be done while brushing one's teeth in the morning, in the subway on the way to work, washing the dishes, hiking in the woods, or shoveling manure in a barn. Prayers can be spoken aloud, sung in choir, or thought in silence. If there is a single element that is most important, it is that of communicating with a higher power. All that one needs to do to get full benefit of the prayer is to start with, "God, I hope you are there and are listening."

Belief in God helps, but it is not essential. Easily overlooked in step 11 is the primary action verb in the step, *sought*. The eleventh step is a step of *seeking*, not necessarily of finding. Prayer and meditation are the activities employed in the process of seeking. Steve's story is instructive. In Steve's story, he talks about considering himself to be an atheist, but because his sponsor advised him to get on his knees and say prayers every morning, that is what he has done for more than thirty years, every day. He has not had an experience of being "heard," but at the same time, neither has he taken a drink. Fundamentally, prayer involves two separate actions: talking and listening. For many people, the listening action occurs primarily during meditation, about which I will speak presently.

By this time in the heroic quest for recovery, the heroes have hopefully developed something of a relationship with their higher power. They have early on come to the hopeful conclusion that God can restore them to sanity and have experienced success on their journey that has vastly exceeded their expectations.

Implicit in the action of talking is the idea that someone is listening. For those for whom the higher power is more abstract than a deity who might be able to listen, prayer does not make as much sense as it does to those who have a more conventional idea of God as "our Father who art in heaven." The advice from their sponsors should be, as in Steve's case, to pray anyway. Sometimes the development of regular prayer times and habits leads to God becoming less of an abstract idea. As Martin Buber says in *Hasidism and Modern Man*, "In our prayers themselves God lets Himself be found."[10]

The results of prayer are often unexpected and sometimes powerful. Most of the time, when people pray, if nothing else, they get some quiet time to themselves and a sense that they just engaged in a worthwhile and purposeful activity. The step calls for the specific action of seeking conscious contact with a higher power. The action of *seeking* is something anyone can do, even if what is sought may not be found just at that time. However, sometimes the results of a prayer are dramatic. Bill Wilson had a profound spiritual experience, a feeling that he was on a mountaintop as a heavenly wind rushed by, accompanied by an experience of euphoria. But one should not judge the benefit of prayer by its immediate results. Some people expect God to answer their prayers directly, giving them advice spoken in their native language. One of the difficulties some alcoholics had during their involvement with the Oxford Group was the Oxford practice of prayer, in which the members kept a pencil and a pad of paper next to themselves to write down the messages received directly from God.

People often think of praying as asking God for some situation to work out in their favor: healing of a loved one from an illness, getting a desired job, not having to sleep outside for another night, having a child, or some other such thing of legitimate importance. Such prayers *are* important, but one's prayer life should include seeking God's will. Rabbi Abraham Twerski writes, "Prayer is a vehicle for bringing us closer to God. The highest aspiration we can have is to stand in close relationship to God. When this is the intent of prayer, it indicates that we have risen far above our personal interests, and that the latter have been displaced by the desire to be close to God."[11] Accordingly, if we pray, we feel closer to God. Note that it is we who must take the action to initiate this closeness, not God. Rabbi Twerski adds,

> Praying for the knowledge of the Divine will for us is edifying, because it reinforces the conviction that we have an important function in the universe. In contrast to the prayer for things that we ask from God, which is our awareness of things *we need*, this knowledge of His will for us is an assertion of our awareness that *we are needed.* . . . It is through prayer, and particularly through prayer for the knowledge of God's will for us and the ability to fulfill that will, that we come to a true spiritual awakening.[12]

Thus, the spiritual awakening is the result of (1) the awareness that we have value; (2) the belief that God does indeed have a will for us, personally; (3) the belief that we can gain knowledge of God's will for us; and (4) the faith that he will grant us the power to carry out his will. Rev. Sam Shoemaker says, "Prayer, mind you, is not an effort to affect the will of God but to discover it."[13]

Self-searching prior to prayer connects the tenth step of self-examination to the eleventh step of prayer and meditation. As Bill Wilson states in *Twelve Steps and Twelve Traditions*, "There is a direct linkage among self-examination, meditation, and prayer. Taken separately, these practices can bring much relief and benefit. But when they are logically related and interwoven, the result is an unshakeable foundation for life."[14]

One important aspect of being honest in prayer is being willing to express our anger with God. Things may happen to us on our journeys in life that we believe to be unfair, wrong, or hurtful to innocent people, and we may develop a big resentment with God. A prime illustration of this is found in the Hebrew Bible in the Book of Job. Job suffers with the loss of his family, his wealth, and his health. He considers the cause to be an act of God, which he believes to be unfair, given that he has always loved God, praised Him, and conducted himself in a virtuous manner. What is worse, his so-called friends visit him and tell him that he must deserve all the misery that has come upon him. What is even worse, although Job does not know this, is that everything that has happened to Job happened because of a bet that God made with Satan that Job would not turn against him, no matter what. Job is angry and demands a hearing from God:

> If only I knew where to find him;
> If only I could go to his dwelling!
> I would state my case before him
> And fill my mouth with arguments.[15]

How many of us have felt like this? I certainly have. Eventually Job gets his hearing and states his case, and the best he can get out of God is, to sum it up, "I am God, and you are not." This response may not seem to be very satisfying, but Job was satisfied to be acknowledged, if not heard. Job accepted his misfortune as God's will, even though he did not understand it.

Everyone on the heroic journey at some time or other will wonder what God was thinking when He let some tragedy happen. If Job got a bad deal in this tale (even if he did get a new family and wealth), I think God does, as well. God has been represented to us as all-powerful, and yet we have free will. We tend to blame God when bad things happen. My grandfather stopped believing in God after the Holocaust. Other people stayed mad at God for the rest of their lives. Some people will never be satisfied with attempts to vindicate God.

The explanation that has worked best for me is from Rabbi Harold Kushner in his book *When Bad Things Happen to Good People* (mentioned by Steve in his story). He and his wife had a child who had a very rare disease in which he failed to develop normally, aged prematurely, and died in his mid teens. Rabbi Kushner struggled to find a justification for this, given the innocence of his son and, for that matter, the sincere effort that he and his wife had made to live virtuous lives. Rabbi Kushner says,

> The idea that God gives people what they deserve, that our misdeeds cause our misfortune, is a neat and attractive solution to the problem of evil at several levels, but it has a number of serious limitations. As we have seen, it teaches people to blame themselves. It creates guilt even where there is no basis for guilt. It makes people hate God, even as it makes them hate themselves. And most disturbing of all, it does not even fit the facts.[16]

He goes on to say,

> Christianity introduced the world to the idea of a God who suffers, alongside the image of a God who creates and commands. Postbiblical Judaism also occasionally spoke of a God who suffers, of a God who is homeless and goes into exile along with His exiled people, a God who weeps when He sees what some of His children are doing to others of His children. I don't know what it means for God to suffer. I don't believe that God is a person like me, with real eyes and real tear ducts to cry, and real nerve endings to feel pain. But I would like to think that the anguish I feel when I read of the sufferings of innocent people reflects God's anguish and God's compassion, even if His way of feeling pain is different from ours. I would like to think that He is the source of my being able feel sympathy and outrage, and that He and I are on the same side when we stand with the victim against those who would hurt him.[17]

In my opinion, nothing has ever been said better. Moreover, Rabbi Kushner could never have come to this point in his thinking and belief without having spent much time both in suffering and in prayer. The illness and death of his son called on him to be heroic, and he accepted the challenge. In the process, he was able to comfort millions of people, myself included.

The problem of suffering is a difficult one. My belief is that there is no explanation that will satisfy everyone. I often hear people tell a person in deep pain that God won't give them more than they can handle. They are telling people that they are stronger than they think they are, that they are there to support them, and that they will come out the other side a stronger and wiser person. This is all well, but I have a problem with the idea that God is giving people problems. This is in fact what happens in the Job story.

I do not believe it is what happens in real life. The idea that God is up there looking down to see to whom He can teach what lesson just does not work for me. It says that we can blame God for our troubles and that we are supposed to understand and forgive God because it is somehow designed to be for our benefit. I just do not believe God is up there pulling strings. God is the effect, not the cause of our troubles. In pain, we seek God, who is always there if we let Him in. This is what works for me. You do not have to agree.

Sometimes it is helpful to read or recite a prayer that someone else has written. These prayers have proven to inspire, to be meaningful, and at times to help facilitate a sense of community within a group. I take the liberty of including a few such prayers here. The reader may feel free to make use of them or not.

The Serenity Prayer

This prayer was adopted by AA in 1942 and has been used ever since. It is often recited in its short form at the beginning or sometimes at the end of an AA meeting, in unison by the group. The author is Reinhold Niebuhr, an eminent Christian writer and theologian (1892–1971). The prayer has great import for AA members as a source of wisdom, comfort, and inspiration on the daily road of the heroic journey of recovery:

> God, grant me the serenity to accept the things I cannot change; courage to change the things I can; and the wisdom to know the difference.

It seemed counterintuitive to me, when I first saw this prayer, that serenity would lead to acceptance of the things that were out of my control. I would have thought that, if I can accept things as they are, then I would become serene. The prayer, though, has it the other way around. If I let God put me at peace, then I can accept what I cannot change. And being at peace for me involved putting myself in God's hands, to the extent that I was able to do so at that time.

Through prayer, our heroes can come to understand the importance of surrendering their will and ego to their higher power. It is through the surrendering of the will and the letting go of the ego that the heroic quest is ultimately achieved.

Acceptance in the sense in which I use it here describes a state in which a difficult situation is acknowledged. As Bill Wilson says in

Language of the Heart, "Our very first problem is to accept our present circumstances as they are, ourselves as we are, and the people about us as they are. This is to adopt a realistic humility without which no genuine advance can ever begin."[18] And as Stephanie Covington says in *A Woman's Way through the Twelve Steps*, "As we accept ourselves and others, as we let go of destructive relationships, of control, of emotional attachment, we develop our capacity for authentic and intimate relationships with ourselves and others."[19]

Accepting what the hero cannot change in this moment is made possible through development of a sense of peace in the moment. However, it does not absolve the hero from taking action when it is called for. Such action involves an honest appraisal of the situation, an honest assessment of one's own motives, discussion with trusted spiritual mentors, and humble consultation with one's higher power. Our hero must seek guidance and courage, decide what is right, and let go of the outcome. As William L. White says in *Slaying the Dragon*, "Slaying the dragon . . . begins with waging war against our flawed selves and ends with the capacity to move forward through the acceptance and transcendence of our own imperfection."[20] This makes it clear that what needs to be accepted most importantly is the interior journey itself. If we accept this challenge and accept the guidance that is offered, then we move in the direction of wholeness and union with our higher power.

Courage has been called for on every step of the twelve step journey, even the first step. Was it not fear that kept the potential heroes from admitting defeat? Once this was accomplished, the road to recovery has involved facing themselves fearlessly (or fearfully) repeatedly. By now, our heroes have adopted a manner of living that includes a relationship with their higher power.

As relationships go, it is challenging because communication is indirect. They have not sat down with God at Starbucks for a latte and conversation. Yet progress has been made, as they have, at an experiential level, felt the beginnings of faith, trust, and confidence in their higher power in the face of life's uncertainties and difficulties—progress that could only be achieved through commitment to prayer and meditation in the daily heroic life.

In the Serenity Prayer, we ask for the wisdom to know the difference between letting something be and deciding to take action. We have already seen that one of the fruits of the program as stated in the Ninth Step Promises is "We will intuitively know how to handle situations which used to baffle us."[21] The experience of walking with God thus far on the heroic journey has changed the heroes in ways that were unexpected and even in ways that they were unaware of until good judgment was called for, and they discovered that they could made a sound decision.

And yet there is a level of mystery and unknowableness about the world that surpasses the imagination. In *Sermon on the Mount*, Emmet Fox says, "God is love, but God is also infinite intelligence, and unless these two qualities are balanced in our lives, we do not get wisdom; for wisdom *is the perfect blending of intelligence and love*."[22] In *God in Search of Man*, Rabbi Heschel looks to Ecclesiastes for understanding: "This is one of Ecclesiastes' central insights: 'I have seen the task that God has given to the sons of men. . . . He has made all things beautiful in its time; but he has also *implanted in the minds of men the mystery*, so that man cannot find out what God has done from the beginning to the end.'"[23] Thus, at some fundamental level, as discussed previously, God is unknowable. Rabbi Heschel continues, "Ecclesiastes is not only saying that the world's wise are not wise enough, but something more radical. What *is*, is more than what you see; what *is*, is 'far off and deep, exceedingly deep' (Ecclesiastes 7:24). *Being is mysterious*."[24]

In search of acceptance and wisdom, I turn again to the Book of Job, which attempts to answer questions about God that have challenged men since the time of their first spiritual awareness many thousands of years ago. There we find, "Do not say, 'we have found wisdom.'"[25] How many times in how many situations do people say to themselves, "I need to figure this out"? At some point, we must accept that there is a mystery that is beyond our capacity to solve or comprehend.

In a chapter by Arthur S. Peake entitled "Job's Victory," we find,

> But since we know God we can trust him to the uttermost; we know, in-credible though it may seem, that the world's misery does not contradict the love of God. It was therefore with deliberate intent that the poet put on God's lips no hint of the reason of Job's suffering. To trust God when we understand Him would be but a sorry triumph for religion. To trust God, when we have every reason for distrusting Him, save our inward certainty of Him, is the supreme victory of religion."[26]

This, indeed, is the epitome of acceptance.

The most painful feeling of most people when they are at their lowest point is that of being alone, of being abandoned, especially being abandoned by God. The painful thought is "I am such a bad person that

I must deserve to be alone; I am unlovable." In Nahum Glatzer's *The Dimensions of Job*, there is a chapter by H. H. Rowley, who says,

> By insisting that there is such a thing as innocent suffering, the author of *Job* is bringing a message of the first importance to the sufferer. The hardest part of his suffering need not be the feeling that he is deserted by God, or the fear that all men will regard him as cast out from God's presence. If his suffering is innocent it may not spell isolation from God, and when he most needs the sustaining presence of God he may still have it. Here is a religious message of great significance.[27]

Of course, unlike Job, we all know that we are guilty of something and believe that we deserve punishment. The great discovery of the heroes on their journeys is that it is not God's desire to punish; rather, what God wants is for us to return to Him in love. And this is what the heroes want, as well—even if they don't know it: to never have to feel alone again.

This brings us back to acceptance, and the heroes are at peace because they realize that this is enough. Vernon J. Bourke in *Augustine's Quest for Wisdom* says,

> Perhaps the greatest lesson that Augustine has to teach is that wisdom and true happiness are not to be bought, or handed over by other creatures like chattel, but is solely the result of divinely aided, personal effort. Each man may reach a different degree of understanding of his own nature and its destiny—such understanding is always the culmination and somewhat solitary quest for wisdom. One may be helped by others. . . . But it is not from other men that wisdom comes. Contemplative repose of soul is found only in God.[28]

Thus, the heroes must pray for wisdom and hope to find some measure of it as they travel.

I now include some other prayers that some people have found useful or comforting. Some are suggested to use daily. I hope that one or more of them may be useful to you on your journey.

Many Jewish people say shortly after awakening a prayer in Hebrew called the Modeh Ani. I include this prayer in my own practice. It translates into English as follows:

> I stand before you, living and eternal God,
> With compassion you have restored my soul to me.
> Great is your faithfulness.

In this way, I start my day by seeking conscious contact with the God of my understanding. Another prayer I find useful, especially in the context of life as a heroic journey, is a prayer said at the morning minyan, the prayer service attended by religious Jews every morning. This is the translation from the Hebrew:

> Praised are You Adonai, Master of the Universe, who strengthens our steps.

William James in *The Varieties of Religious Experience* cites a prayer written in the early 1400s. Apparently, seeking God's will is not a new idea: "Lord, thou knowest what is best; let this or that be according as thou wilt, so much as thou wilt, when thou wilt. Do with me as thou knowest best, and as shall be most to thine honour. Place me where thou wilt, and freely work thy will with me in all things."[29] Another traditional prayer is known as the Jesus Prayer: "Lord Jesus Christ, Son of God, have mercy on me, a sinner."

In *Markings*, notes that he wrote to be published after his death, Dag Hammerskjöld writes a brief and lovely prayer:

> Give me a pure heart—that I may see Thee,
> A humble heart—that I may hear Thee,
> A heart of love—that I may serve Thee,
> A heart of faith—that I may abide in Thee.[30]

One of the favorite prayers of AA members is known as the Prayer of St. Francis. It is cited in *Twelve Steps and Twelve Traditions* as a good example of a prayer as a starting place for those who are unfamiliar with the practice of prayer—or for anyone else, for that matter. Bill Wilson also suggests that the ideas expressed would be useful to meditate on. While this prayer has been attributed to St. Francis of Assisi, it actually was written much more recently, around 1900 by a French priest:

> Lord, make me an instrument of thy peace—that where there is hatred, I may bring love—that where there is wrong, I may bring the spirit of forgiveness—that where there is discord, I may bring harmony—that where there is error, I may bring truth—that where there is doubt, I may bring faith—that where there is despair, I may bring hope—that where there are shadows, I may bring light—that where there is sadness, I may bring joy. Lord, grant that I may seek rather to comfort than to be comforted—to understand, than to be understood—to love, than to be loved. For it is by

self-forgetting that one finds. It is by forgiving that one is forgiven. It is by dying that one awakens to Eternal Life. Amen."[31]

In the Big Book, we find three prayers that are useful on the heroic journey, one each to be read after taking the third and seventh steps and one to be recited several times every day:

1. The third step prayer: "God, I offer myself to Thee—to build with me and to do with me as Thou wilt. Relieve me of the bondage of self, that I may better do Thy will. Take away my difficulties, that victory over them may bear witness to those I would help of Thy Power, Thy Love, and Thy Way of Life. May I do Thy will always!"[32]
2. The seventh step prayer: "My Creator, I am now willing that You should have all of me, good and bad. I pray that You now remove from me every single defect of character which stands in the way of my usefulness to You and my fellows. Grant me strength, as I go out from here, to do Your bidding. Amen."[33]
3. And finally, the prayer to be said several times per day: "Thy will be done."[34]

In *Drop the Rock*, Bill P., Todd W., and Sara S. offer their own seventh-step prayer:

> God (or Higher Power), thank You for the gift of my recovery and for all the benefits in my life. Please allow me to be open and grateful for the bounty of friends, family, growth, and much more in my life. Please help me gain an awareness of those shortcomings that hinder my service to others, myself, and You. Please help me find a way to remove those character defects in my life, both the ones I'm currently aware of and those that I may gain awareness of later. Help me become who and what I may become, in order to give more. Amen.[35]

Here is a prayer from Father Thomas Merton, as quoted by Buddhist author William Alexander:

> My Lord God, I have no idea where I am going. I do not see the road ahead of me. I cannot know for certain where it will end. Nor do I really know myself, and the fact that I think I am following your will does not mean that I am actually doing so. But I believe that the desire to please you does in fact please you. And I hope that I will not ever do anything

apart from that desire. And I know that if I do this you will lead me by the right road, though I may know nothing about it. Therefore I will trust you always though I may seem to be lost and in the shadow of death. I will not fear, for you are ever with me, and you will never leave me to face my perils alone.[36]

The Psalms are a gold mine of spiritual sustenance. Here are a couple selections:

Psalm 51:10–12

Create in me a pure heart, O God,
And renew a steadfast spirit within me
Do not cast me from your presence
Or take your Holy Spirit from me
Restore to me the joy of your salvation
And grant me a willing spirit, to sustain me.[37]

Psalm 56:3–4

When I am afraid, I put my trust in you.
In God, whose word I praise—
In God I trust and am not afraid.[38]

Alcoholics Anonymous has adopted what is commonly known as the Lord's Prayer. Roman Catholics refer to the prayer as the Our Father. The prayer is typically recited at the end of every AA meeting, although there are exceptions. While there are those who are uncomfortable with saying a prayer from Christian scripture at AA, which is nonreligious and nondenominational, every group has the choice of what, if any, prayers will be said at the group meeting. The prayer itself is in the words of Jesus, a Jewish preacher, who is teaching a moral lesson about living according to God's will and about forgiveness:

This, then, is how you should pray:

Our Father in heaven,
Hallowed be your name,
Your kingdom come,
Your will be done,
On earth as it is in heaven.
Give us today our daily bread.
And forgive us our debts,

As we also have forgiven our debtors,
And lead us not into temptation,
But deliver us from the evil one.[39]

The prayer recited at AA is typically the King James translation. Verse 13 differs significantly in the last two lines from the previous NIV version. It reads,

And lead us not into temptation but deliver us from evil:
For thine is the kingdom, and the power, and the glory, forever, Amen.

Unfortunately, many arguments and hard feelings have erupted over prayer practices at AA meetings. Members and groups have always found a way to work these things out, whether by vote of the group, by individuals finding other meetings more to their liking, or by some dissatisfied members starting a new group. There are secular AA groups where God is not mentioned by name. These are serious discussions when they occur, and everyone deserves to be heard. All disputes within AA groups are resolved by what is referred to as group conscience, a practice formulated in tradition 2 of the twelve traditions: "For our group purpose there is but one ultimate authority—a loving God as He may express Himself in our group conscience. Our leaders are but trusted servants: they do not govern."[40] Thus far, AA has not come close to being destroyed by religious wars.

If prayer can be thought of as talking to God, then possibly meditation can be thought of as listening to God. Meditation as a practice is surging in the Western world. While Eastern culture and religion have always been familiar with meditation, in the West, it is still foreign to most people. Growing up in Chicago, attending public schools, and going to synagogue, I understood that people prayed, but I don't know that I ever thought about meditation one way or the other. My first exposure to meditation was when I bought a mantra and took very brief training in Transcendental Meditation, a practice promoted by a man who called himself the Maharishi Mahesh Yogi, which was popularized when the Beatles took it up. They subsequently soured on him and wrote a song, "Sexy Sadie," satirizing him. I gave the practice a try when I was in my early thirties, but I found it impossible to meditate for twenty minutes at a time, let alone do it twice daily. The practice itself was also difficult for me. I don't think that, until this time in the early 1970s, I was able to make a clear distinction between prayer and meditation.

Meditation can be done in several ways. There are many books on the subject, and classes can be taken. While much of what is written in popular literature relates to Buddhist practice, especially mindfulness meditation, it is not at all necessary to meditate as a religious practice. Meditation is not worship. There are methods of meditation practiced in all religions that I know of, although in some religions, the practice is limited largely to monastics.

In the most basic sense, meditation is a way of focusing on the present moment. This may be accomplished through some sort of breathing exercise. In this way, the individual can get centered and block out the noise from the outside. At the same time, one recognizes that most of the noise comes from inside. People who engage in meditation will quickly find themselves losing focus and thinking about anything and everything else. When this happens, once the distraction is recognized, meditators quietly bring themselves back to their center and their breathing. It is important to be nonjudgmental about lack of focus. Jon Kabat-Zinn lists seven attitudes that the meditator brings to the practice: (1) nonjudging, (2) patience, (3) beginner's mind, (4) trust, (5) nonstriving, (6) acceptance (!), and (7) letting go.[41] He describes breathing exercises that can be used in mindfulness meditation.

Thich Nhat Hanh, in *Living Buddha, Living Christ*, says, "Conscious breathing is the most basic Buddhist practice for touching peace."[42] He offers a simple technique for a beginner. The meditator sits in a comfortable, relaxed position and thinks to himself,

> Breathing in, I calm my body.
> Breathing out, I smile.
> Dwelling in the present moment,
> I know this is a wonderful moment.[43]

This is done slowly, calmly, comfortably, for as long as is desired, as often as desired.

My own practice is to focus on the area of my heart and upper abdomen, thinking of the words *soft* and *quiet* as I do so. I breathe slowly, inhaling comfortably, letting the air out, and quietly waiting until I feel the need to take another breath. I do not make a point of breathing deeply. If I feel tension or pain or, my most common distraction, itching anywhere in my body, I recognize that my attention has been drawn away from my center, and I quietly return. When I find myself thinking about something else, I quietly return to my breathing and my center. I have found that with this practice my body grows quiet, as does my mind, at least for short periods of time. It is comforting and refreshing.

Many people use some form of yoga as a meditation practice. Another form of meditation is to meditate on a word or phrase, repeating it over and over. Such a word or phrase might be *peace* or *world peace* or a religious-themed phrase or name. Regardless of practice, usually both the mind and body are involved. Whatever method you try, I suggest that you stay with it until it is second nature to you. If a method is not working, try something else. It may be worthwhile to get an instructor to help you. And you can learn to do anything on YouTube.

I devote more space in this chapter to prayer than to meditation, probably a reflection more of my greater familiarity with prayer than meditation as far as I have traveled on my journey to this point. Do not take it as an indication that meditation is less important. As noted earlier, conscious contact with our higher power, if I can oversimplify for the moment, involves both talking and listening, sending and receiving— and both prayer and meditation equally and in their own ways facilitate this communication. Do give both equal weight and effort, and your results will cause you to "be amazed before you are half-way through."[44]

STEP 12: "HAVING HAD A SPIRITUAL AWAKENING AS THE RESULT OF THESE STEPS, WE TRIED TO CARRY THIS MESSAGE TO ALCOHOLICS, AND TO PRACTICE THESE PRINCIPLES IN ALL OUR AFFAIRS."[45]

There are three components to the twelfth step: (1) spiritual awakening, (2) carrying the message, and (3) practicing the principles in all one's affairs. The heroes have returned to their native land, the kingdom, sober and armed with new self-awareness, newfound wisdom, and inspiration to help others who need what they have. Now transformed, they nevertheless must continue their journeys but in a new phase, where they must help others and live righteously in order to maintain their renewed spiritual selves.

Let us consider what it means to have a spiritual awakening. In the Big Book, the terms *spiritual awakening* and *spiritual experience* are both used somewhat interchangeably. In the section "Spiritual Experience" in appendix 2 of the Big Book, we find, "Most of us think this *awareness* of a Power greater than ourselves is the essence of spiritual experience. Our more religious members call it 'God-consciousness.'"[46] The idea of an awakening is self-explanatory. I have come to define *spiritual awakening* as the discovery of oneself as a beautiful, intelligent, worthwhile, and lovable person, a child of God. In *Twelve Steps and Twelve Traditions*, Bill Wilson says there are many definitions of *spiritual awakening* but then goes on to propose his own:

> When a man or a woman has a spiritual awakening, the most important meaning of it is that he has now become able to do, feel, and believe that which he could not do before on his unaided strength and resources alone. He has been granted a gift which amounts to a new state of consciousness and being. He has been set on a path which tells him he is really going somewhere, that life is not a dead end, not something to be endured or mastered. In a very real sense he has been transformed because he has laid hold of a source of strength which, in one way or another, he had hitherto denied himself. He finds himself in possession of a degree of honesty, tolerance, unselfishness, peace of mind, and love of which he had thought himself quite incapable.[47]

In other terms, for Jung, the hero has reached the state of individuation; for Campbell, it is wholeness; for the Christian, it is union with Christ. Call it what you will, but it is real. And please note again Bill's use of the metaphor of a journey. Importantly, all this has come about as the result of the first eleven steps. When Bill says, "Having had a spiritual awakening as the result of these steps," the twelfth step had not yet formally been taken. Having taken the first eleven steps, the traveler is already transformed. The twelfth step consolidates, solidifies, maintains, and advances what has already been accomplished. Now that the heroes have come home, they have work to do.

Returning to the idea of the heroic journey, the heroes have seen that it is a quest for oneself, a serious seeking deeply within, a rooting out of all the dishonesty, arrogance, false pride, anger, and fear. It is nothing other than a spiritual quest for the God within. The heroic journey is about learning to love oneself, love one's fellow man, and love the God of their understanding. They have discovered a world of wonder and hopefulness that they never suspected existed, and they found that they could not have even attempted, let alone successfully taken this journey, without spiritual guidance. They have seen that their prior life consisted of running from themselves in fear and hating what they had become at those times when they even dared to look.

From such a place of dread, terror, and rage had they come, slowly allowing themselves to be guided, to risk taking each next step on the journey, until "sometimes quickly, sometimes slowly," they found themselves transformed.[48] The heroes have discovered, unexpectedly, that the journey they have been on has taken them to an unexpected destination we may call *spiritually awake*. Travelers to Chicago will get on the train labeled "Chicago," and when they arrive, they will be in Chicago. Alcoholics who embark on the twelve step journey at first expect that, when they arrive at their destination, they will be at "Sober." For some this is as far as they get, and if so, there is a great risk of backsliding because, for some people, *sober* only means *dry*. The spiritual awakening is the result of the interior heroic journey as guided by the twelve steps. No journey, no transformation.

What strikes me as the most remarkable of all the words and ideas expressed in the Big Book is what the twelfth step does not say. The twelfth step does not say, "Having *stayed sober* as the result of these steps." One could have expected exactly that. Instead, it says, "Having had a spiritual awakening as *the* result of these steps."[49] The word *the* is used, as though the spiritual awakening was the singular purpose of the journey. It is not "having had a spiritual awakening as *a* result, among many results, of these steps." No, it is that *the result of the steps is a spiritual awakening.*

Of course, this could never have happened while drinking or other addictive behaviors continued, so sobriety is certainly a prime benefit of the steps, but the objective of the journey, although at the outset the hero did not realize it, was a spiritual awakening. There is not much chance that the heroes would have attempted this journey in the first place if they knew where the train was going. By practicing the twelve steps, the heroes discover that it is worthwhile every day to think about where they are in life and where they are headed on their heroic, spiritual journey. In his 1916 poem "Limited," Carl Sandburg portrays this idea:

I am riding on a limited express, one of the crack trains of the nation.
Hurtling across the prairie into blue haze and dark air go fifteen all-steel
Coaches holding a thousand people.
(All the coaches shall be scrap and rust and all the men and women
Laughing in the diners and sleepers shall pass to ashes.)
I ask a man in the smoker where he is going and he answers: "Omaha."[50]

The theme of being useful appears frequently in Bill Wilson's writing. Service to others is widely understood as an important goal in life. Dr. Albert Schweitzer says, "I don't know what your destiny will be, but one thing I know; the only ones among you who will be really happy are those who have sought and found how to serve."[51] While Bill never limits good works to helping other alcoholics, this is his primary focus.

In the common jargon of AA, if a member "twelfth-steps" someone, they are calling on a drinker in need. This is using *twelfth-step* as a verb. For Bill Wilson, he knew that it was crucial from the very first day of his sobriety that he help others. It was one of the very first thoughts after he came down from the "mountaintop" of what he referred to as the "hot flash" he experienced on his fourth and last admission to Towns Hospital. He commenced to visit alcoholics in bars and in detox, sharing his spiritual experience, telling people that he had been released from his compulsion to drink. In the first five months, the only alcoholic he helped was himself.

With guidance from Dr. William Silkworth, he refined his method and message and within days was confronted with a do-or-die situation. Out of town on a failed business trip, he felt a strong urge to drink. Having experienced the benefit of talking with another alcoholic in such a circumstance, he acted. He made a few phone calls, and by the next day, he was face-to-face with another man who drank like he used to, Dr. Bob Smith. Smith also quit drinking immediately, although there was one more binge a few weeks later. Having no program as such, they worked with what they had: the belief that God had released them from their compulsion to drink and that, in order to stay sober, they had to carry what they had found to others. From just such humble and unlikely beginnings came a fellowship that more than eighty-five years later numbers more than two million members and is showing no signs of losing steam.

James Baldwin in *The Fire Next Time* says, "To accept one's past—one's history—is not the same thing as drowning in it; it is learning how to use it."[52] In the Big Book, Bill Wilson presents his statement of purpose, his primary reason for being: "Our real purpose is to fit ourselves to be of maximum service to God and the people about us."[53] Bill Wilson was of maximum service sobering up alcoholics and ensuring the long-term viability and success of Alcoholics Anonymous.

The spiritual awakening makes it clear to the heroes that, having obtained their treasure, they need to share it with others. A Chasidic saying goes, "If you don't involve yourself in the Exodus today, tomorrow you will be back in Egypt." Dr. Bob Smith addressed the first international convention of AA in Cleveland in 1950. He was very ill with cancer and died not long thereafter. He said,

> Our Twelve Steps, when simmered down to the last, resolve themselves into the words "love" and "service." We understand what love is, and we understand what service is. So, let's bear those two things in mind. . . . And one more thing: None of us would be here today if somebody hadn't taken the time to explain things to us, to give us a little pat on the back, to take us to a meeting or two, to do numerous little kind and thoughtful acts in our behalf. So let us never get such a degree of smug complacency that we're not willing to extend, or attempt to extend, to our less fortunate brothers that help which has been so beneficial to us.[54]

Refusal to respond to the call and refusal to return home with the treasure are the negative elements of the heroic journey that either can prevent a potential hero from finding the hero within or can cause the hero to step off the path. Failure to work the recovery program of AA risks relapse into active drinking. Just coming to meetings with no working of the steps can keep a person dry for a while, but sobriety (soundness of mind) remains elusive. Every alcoholic, whether sober one day or forty years, is at arm's length from the next drink.

Regrettably, many who enter AA and work the program to great effect eventually drop away. They cut back on meeting attendance. They stop calling their sponsors. They get out of the habits of self-awareness (step 10) and spiritual awareness (step 11). Then they stop going to meetings altogether. They have stopped working with others and slowly stop living according to the spiritual principles that brought them into recovery. They have left the path, quit the heroic journey. What they will lose first is what I call emotional sobriety, and they regress into what some in AA call "sodriety"—dry but not sober. Too often a drink follows, with the predictable progressive course that leads to what brought them to the program in the first place.

The path can be abandoned at any point along the way for those who do make the attempt at traversing it. Some fail to acknowledge any sort of power greater than themselves. Deflation of the prideful ego is not accomplished. Such people usually drop out early, but some stay on, remaining sober on the fellowship while not working steps, sometimes for long stretches of time. Some acknowledge that there must be a higher power but are unwilling to surrender. Others make a surrender, at least of sorts, but fail to embark on a fearless and searching moral inventory of themselves. In this way, the person fails to engage in the inner journey of self-discovery and self-love. It is frequently at this point that people stop coming to meetings.

Many people who quit AA and have not (yet) relapsed believe that they no longer need the program. They feel happy and stable in their relationships and may even attend church regularly. What they do not consider is that a basic ingredient in staying sober is working with other alcoholics. This was among the first things that Bill Wilson knew the day of his own sudden spiritual awakening: If he wanted to keep it, then he would have to give it away. So, people who "graduate" from AA abandon a basic element of recovery. And even if they do stay sober and enjoy happy and useful lives, by not attending meetings they deprive many people of the help that may have made the difference in their lives.

In the introduction to *The Power of Myth*, Joseph Campbell says, "The ultimate aim of the quest must be neither release nor ecstasy for oneself, but the wisdom and power to serve others."[55] One of the many distinctions between the celebrity and the hero, he said, is that "one lives only for self while the other acts to redeem society."[56] To *redeem society*? Yes, that is what he said. If that sounds grandiose, then it simply reflects the degree of importance our responsibility is to others—the responsibility of heroes to share their treasure each day with the person who may need it.

The final task of the hero is to practice the principles in all affairs. Many people translate this as "Do the next right thing." This does not have to be confusing; an AA slogan is "Keep It Simple." Each day our heroes think a thousand thoughts and does a thousand things. They feel their feelings a thousand times per day. Through all these mostly little events, they must maintain themselves in a fit spiritual condition so that, when something negative appears in their minds, they can correct it quickly. Some days nothing happens to require a major decision. However, by staying on the path, practicing the steps each day, when a major decision is called for, they will "intuitively know how to handle" the situation.

My father, Moses Gordon, used to say that when he and my mother married, they made an agreement. She would make all the minor decisions, and he would make all the major decisions. He then would pause and add, "To date, there have been no major decisions." A great joke, but it does illustrate a point. "There are no big deals" is another statement frequently heard in the AA rooms. Sometimes there is doubt about the "next right thing." A friend told me that, in his twenty-five years in AA, he had sponsored many men. From time to time, one of these men would call him to ask for advice about a situation that he didn't know how to handle. My friend said that, in every case, without exception, the man really did know what to do. The next right thing is just not that confusing or hard to figure out. However, there are times when talking it over with a sponsor or trusted friend does help clarify issues and give a person confidence that he is making the right decision.

One could become overwhelmed at the idea that, for the rest of one's life, it will be necessary to practice these steps all day, every day. It can seem like a burden, but in reality, it is the opposite. The overriding principle is taking things as they come, one day at a time. The original application of "one day at a time" was in not taking a drink one day at a time. When AA members are craving a drink, this principle can still be lifesaving. Just put the drink off until tomorrow. Get through today sober. Taken further, the principle of living in the now has great spiritual merit. Put simply, this moment is the heroes' only opportunity to spend with God, to repair the world, to love their fellow man or woman or themselves.

Rabbi Heschel writes, "It takes three things to attain a sense of significant being: God, A Soul, and A Moment. And the three are always here."[57] To me, this is profound in its simplicity and as powerful an understanding of a spiritual experience as I have found. He makes this very simple in a down-to-earth way, which makes the idea seem more like practical living and less like deep philosophy. And we find in the Big Book,

It is easy to let up on our program of spiritual action and rest on our laurels. We are headed for trouble if we do, for alcohol is a subtle foe. We are not cured of alcoholism. What we really have is a daily reprieve contingent on the maintenance of our spiritual condition. Every day is a day when we must carry the vision of God's will into all of our activities. "How can I best serve Thee—Thy will [not mine] be done."[58]

And as my friend Dick S. likes to point out, the daily reprieve is contingent on the *maintenance* of our spiritual condition. It requires action. It is not the sparkling clean floor but rather the mopping of the floor that is our focus and responsibility.

By living in today, the hero, for the moment, can dispense with regrets and resentment of the past and with worries about the future. Eckhart Tolle writes, "All negativity is caused by an accumulation of psychological time and denial of the present. Unease, anxiety, tension, stress, worry—all forms of fear—are caused by too much future, and not enough presence. Guilt, regret, resentment, grievances, sadness, bitterness, and all forms of non-forgiveness are caused by too much past, and not enough presence."[59]

A phrase often heard in Al-Anon is "Let go of the outcome." Once our heroes realize that the outcome is not up to themselves, a great sense of relief is experienced. For those who have lived in dread of what is going to happen next due to the uncontrolled drinking of a loved one, it is a great relief to finally comprehend that, as hard as they might try, they are just as powerless over alcohol as the alcoholic. All heroes on this journey come to understand and accept that the future is out of their control. Much time and energy can be devoted to stressing over something that is not even real. Aided by the recovery fellowship and our constant contact with our higher power, walking these steps each day, having compassion for ourselves and our fellows, life can be remarkable, and it can come very close to what it is supposed to be, one day at a time.

James's Story

His Daughters Demanded the Best of Him

My story begins as one of six children growing up in an impoverished single-parent home. I remember my mother working her fingers to the bone just to keep food on the table and a roof over our heads. She taught me what hard work and resilience look like. I am no different from any addict in terms of the emotional trauma that sometimes comes with addiction and in most cases begins in childhood.

My two biggest heroes were my mother-in-law and my wife of twenty-five years. I say that because they were the first people who expressed how much they believed in my ability to succeed. In 1986, I enlisted in the US Navy from my home state of New Jersey. At that time, we had three daughters who were ten, eight, and three years old. The following year, we had our fourth daughter, and for the next ten years, I was aboard ship or traveling around the world. I saw thirteen countries in just four years!

My wife's mother, one of my heroes, died in 1993. This was a very traumatic experience for me. I began to feel abandoned but was still able to somewhat maintain. Then, in 2004, my girls and I lost the love of my life since I was eighteen years old, my dear wife. I could not maintain life at that point and did not know how to process losing my second-biggest hero. I hit a rock bottom of crack cocaine and heroin that I never knew existed.

I spent the next two years in gross addiction, homeless, or in jail. I remember one of my daughters saying to me, "Dad, it's like we lost Mommy and you at the same time." That made me really look at how I made a mess of the hero image with my girls. I applaud my older daughters, who stepped up and became Mom and Dad to their younger sisters

141

at the most difficult time in our lives. My two older daughters refused to accept my addiction and behavior as normal; this was not the loving dad they had grown up with!

They picked me up from a drug-infested hotel and brought me to rehab in 2006. When it was time for me to make the proper amends, I thanked one daughter for kicking me off her couch and the other who found the treatment program for homeless addicts that changed my life. I am so proud because it was their beautiful mother who taught them not to settle for less and to demand the best in a person. They did all they could to help me and did not enable me in my addictions. With their love and support, I have become the man that I am today.

I was graced to be able to come back to same treatment program in 2008 as a volunteer sponsor and mentor after putting my life back together. I had returned to school to pursue my certification in addiction counseling. The grace increased in 2009, as I had the opportunity to do my clinical internship at the very place that saved my life. In March 2010, when the program director called me into his office and offered me a full-time position, I gladly accepted, and the magic continued. I began to touch lives, see the transformations, and watch the reconciliation of families. I saw the smiles and laughter of children and rebirth of their fathers, men who once thought their life was over, just as I had of my own life. They discovered that their past did not define their future.

I found my place in the vision and mission of this amazing organization and the intricate workings of the donors, volunteers, board of directors, and the greatest boss in the world with an immense heart for people. I was a part-time chef to cook dinner for the guys and to celebrate the alumni and their achievements. I enjoyed helping to coordinate our annual Java Jam fundraising event and hosting Lake Day for the residents. I would do whatever it took to keep our vision and mission on fire.

I truly believe that my life struggle pointed me to my purpose in working with broken men. It was my absolute pleasure to do so these last twelve years, amazingly for the last ten years as program director. I believe God is now directing me to accept a new challenge with a new organization as I continue my own journey of recovery and of helping addicted men recover and find their own ways. With all my soul, I am grateful to all the people whom God has put in my path to be a part of who I am today. It is with a mixture of sadness and excitement I look forward to experiencing what God has in store for me on this incredible journey.

Charles's Story

The Valedictorian Is Humbled

My early recollections of preteen years were of feeling self-conscious. I would compensate by being aggressive in sports and always having an excuse for unacceptable behavior. At fifteen, I found the solution to my insecurity: beer. I had unlimited access from my dad's supply. Ironically, I had a large capacity, and for years, I was able to function well with a few beers after school or work.

I decided to marry my longtime girlfriend at twenty-one. Neither of us had a clue as to what marriage involved. I was emotionally a fifteen-year-old. For the next twenty years, I was able to graduate from college and medical school and finish a long surgical residency, including two years in the Army Medical Corps. Several beers after work sufficed. We had three children in the '60s, and as my work stress increased, so did my sense of isolation, and my dependence on alcohol progressed.

In my early forties, my wife left me, taking my ten-year-old son away and leaving me with two teenagers. My resentment over this event increased my alcohol use. The next ten years I definitely crossed the line into full-blown alcoholism. I have never been able to fully repair the relationships with my children.

I subsequently married a younger woman who was an addict. This was a very painful phase of my personal and professional life. The loss of my family and the effects of alcoholism created a very dark and threatening outlook on life for me. As a busy surgeon, these years were filled with fear and, at times, terror. By the grace of God, I had no arrests or patient accidents. I had to have medication, legal or illegal, on most days.

We had a child in 1983, and my drug use decreased, but the alcohol consumption rapidly increased. Eventually, I could not drink enough to relieve the cravings and had to use more substances to attempt to function. In 1985, my hospital intervened. I went to outpatient treatment, but I used throughout. I went into treatment at the hospital where I was on staff. Nearing the graduation date, I appointed myself valedictorian of the class and sat down one evening with a bottle of wine to write my speech. I was intoxicated at the ceremony, to the point where it culminated in my being locked up on the psychiatric ward—at my hospital, of course. Fortunately, I remember very little of the actual events. I spent the next six months as an inpatient at several treatment centers.

I was finally able to comprehend the first step with the love of the program of Alcoholics Anonymous and the help of a patient sponsor. The loss of my medical practice, financial instability, and ultimate divorce from the second marriage left me emotionally distraught. The shame of being an alcoholic had brought me to that place of complete surrender.

Returning home after six months clean and sober, I had to immerse myself in AA. I chose a "drill sergeant" sponsor and struggled through the steps over the next year. Having a home group that I attended daily for many years and being of service eased the stress of early sobriety.

I have been blessed by meeting my current wife of thirty years at my home group when I was three years' sober. My wife and I have had thirty years together in recovery. In our first ten years together, there were many hurdles that I had to face from the wreckage of my past. But once again, the patience and love of my wife and the program of Alcoholics Anonymous sustained me.

The amends process of the eighth and ninth steps came very slowly for me. My relationship with my children was severely compromised, but over the years, most (not all) of the emotional wounds are healing. At times, it still takes a major letting go and trusting in God to get through these moments. My relationship with God has come a long way since the days of my active alcoholism. At some level I wanted to be close to God, but my drinking and its effect on my personality blocked me. The best I could seem to do was sit down late at night with a bottle and glass and listen to Jimmy Swaggart preach on the radio. The promises have slowly come true for me. Today I do not regret the past and do not need to shut the door on it.

After many years together, we were blessed with a miraculous gift, a baby daughter, in 2015. She has been a source of unimaginable joy. During this time of raising a small child, my wife and I have been blessed by the love and direction of our sponsors and the fellowship. I practice daily rituals of prayer and Big Book reading, and I attend several AA meetings per week. I call my sponsor once a week for a tenth step inventory. I thank God for looking after me, as I now know that I can always find something to be grateful for even at my advanced age. Every day I thank God for these many gifts.

Sharing my experience with other alcoholics and particularly with newcomers has been the source of a strong sense of God's presence and has given me tremendous satisfaction. My medical practice over the last thirty years has been another gift, in that it has given me a great sense of purpose and gratitude. Now at eighty-five years of age and thirty-five years into recovery, I need to strengthen all my recovery tools. The pandemic had taken its toll on my meeting attendance. I have had increased apprehension regarding my age and stamina, and so I am excited to be back to live meetings.

My attitude dramatically improves with more personal contact with fellow alcoholics. Sharing the common demons of fear, doubt, and insecurity on a one-to-one basis seems to strengthen my God connection, and serenity usually rapidly follows. What an amazing journey this has been, and I feel so grateful to be a recovering alcoholic. This journey in sobriety has given me my life back and so much joy by God's infinite grace. All I have to do is trust in Him, keep it simple, and not drink today.

Chapter Nine

Learning from the Adventures of Others

Analysis of the Stories

There is magic in storytelling. Listeners are transported into the world of the narrator, imagining themselves in the role of the hero or possibly of the victim of the story. Stories can take on mythical power and significance. They reverberate with archetypal themes, echoing deeply into a person's soul. They inform people about the world, who they are, and what their place is in the world. They bring people together and cement bonds between them. Whether at a family reunion, a barbershop or hair salon, a church gathering, a restaurant, or a neighborhood play outing, what do people do, except entertain themselves and others by telling and listening to stories (and eat)? We read stories in the newspaper or online and see them on television. These can be inspirational, informative, or sometimes disturbing. We watch movies, go to plays, or even read comic books that draw us into the action and the lives of the characters. If stories did not affect us emotionally, then they would be of little interest—just ask Aristotle.

Storytelling is a powerful tradition in Alcoholics Anonymous. When Dr. Bob Smith reluctantly agreed to meet with Bill Wilson at Henrietta Seiberling's home in 1934, he only went to please his wife, as he expected a lecture from some stranger about the evils of drink. He said he would stay fifteen minutes, no more. Instead, Bill Wilson told him his own story of suffering from alcoholism and his own story of recovery. He told Dr. Bob that Bob was doing him a favor. He explained that he felt shaky in his sobriety after his business deal went sour and that he was all alone in Akron, away from his support system. He told Dr. Bob that he had discovered that talking with another alcoholic took away his own urge to drink. Smith was so compelled by Bill Wilson and his story that he stayed five hours and forty-five minutes longer than he had planned. Why was that, if not that he found, for the first time in his own experience, another man who understood what it was like to be an alcoholic—to be compelled to drink despite the consequences? So the very first encounter that led to the formation of a worldwide fellowship of millions of recovering alcoholics began with two men and a story.

Although there are no rules to speak of in AA, there are traditions, including regarding how the AA meetings are generally conducted. One form of meeting is called a speaker's meeting. This type of meeting is designed to help the listener identify with what the speaker's life had been like as a drinker, hear how the speaker came to the point of quitting, and to be inspired by the transformed life. People are invited to "tell their story." Early AA members, even before the group had a name, observed the power of telling their own stories to a prospective member. Every motivational speaker has stories to tell to draw in their audience. Every salesperson connects with their customers with a story.

Bill Wilson, in writing the Big Book, understood the power of a story of recovery. Without the stories, very few people would have believed the rest of what the book had to say. In the first edition of the Big Book and through all the subsequent editions, one finds such stories of addiction, of a turning point, and of recovery through involvement with AA and the twelve steps. In the same section that the twelve steps are presented in the Big Book, we find the simple format described as follows: "Our stories disclose in a general way what we used to be like, what happened, and what we are like now."[1]

This tradition is now carried out every day all over the world in one-to-one calls on alcoholics still out there suffering, as well as at the meetings of Alcoholics Anonymous. The speaker is an invited guest who is asked to tell his own story along the lines of what it was like, what happened, and what it is like now. Sometimes the format calls for the speaker to use the entire hour, leaving no time for discussion. In other meetings, the speaker will talk for twenty to thirty minutes, allowing time for others to respond to the story and say how it affected them. In one meeting style, two or three speakers take their turns at the podium. Sometimes the meeting will take a break and reconvene ten or fifteen minutes later (however long it takes to smoke a cigarette and go to the bathroom). In this style of meeting, there is no clock ticking. The meeting is over once every person who wants to share has had a chance.

Throughout this book are such stories of men and women who have had a terrible period of active addiction in their lives, have succeeded in stopping drinking or drugging, and have found a new way of life. They share these stories, and they talk about what their lives are like now. The stories have been told in their own words, written with their own style. I use these stories to illustrate how each conforms to a heroic journey. I also tell the story of Bill Wilson because he is such a key figure in the development of Alcoholics Anonymous. Finally, I include a story of a biblical hero, the patriarch Jacob. I include a Bible story because of the respect people have for the book itself, because of the inspirational value, and because of the guidance people have found from it for their own lives. I tell of Jacob in particular because his story is one of the most comprehensive in the Hebrew Bible. We know more about Jacob than almost any biblical character. And I tell his story because he had profound spiritual experiences.

Many heroic tales include a story of the miraculous birth of the hero. Earlier, I mentioned the biblical character Moses as an example. He had been rescued from a basket floating in the Nile by Pharaoh's daughter. Another example of miraculous birth is the heroic legend of Katoyis, Blood-clot Boy, the hero in the Blackfoot myth, who originated in a drop of blood remaining from a buffalo hunt. In many heroic myths, the hero is born of a virgin. Romulus and Remus were said to be born of the virgin Rhea Silvia. In Egyptian mythology, Ra, the sun, was born of the virgin goddess Net, and the god Horus was born of the virgin goddess Isis. The goddess Persephone was the virgin mother to both Jason and Dionysius. Jacob was born only after his father, Isaac, prayed to God because his wife Rebecca was unable to conceive. At the time of his birth, he was preceded out of the womb by his twin brother, Esau. Jacob struggled to get out first and even had a grip on Esau's heel as they emerged.

Two of our stories are parodies of this format. Niall was conceived after the family dog Bisno chewed up his mother's diaphragm. For years afterward, this was a family joke, and he was referred to as the "afterbirth." Thus his life script started with ridicule, and to this day, he thinks God laughs at him. Youngblood was given up by her birth mother and maliciously referred to as a "tumor" she had been afflicted with. She experienced a painful childhood of abuse that embittered her for many years and made her very self-destructive.

Let us look at how the heroic journey is played out in the stories in this book. The first element in the classical heroic journey is the call to adventure. The call to the adventure of recovery in the lives of addicts comes many times before it is answered. Addicts have multiple experiences in which they are sick, humiliated, or arrested or have a major consequence of one sort or another that should call attention to the fact that something is terribly wrong and something must be done immediately and definitively. The call to adventure is ultimately the call to face life on life's terms instead of trying to escape from one's inner feelings and oneself.

Seldom do addicts recognize the call for what it is, and therefore we find a refusal of the call repeatedly. In Bill Wilson's case, the call was sometimes ignored and at other times responded to by the determination to work it out himself, just as he had with the boomerang challenge. Hearing stories in which others admit to complete defeat can give people the insight and courage to do the same thing for themselves. Some people refuse the call their entire lives; many do, in fact. That this is a tragedy is attested to by the fact that so many have been successful with the twelve step approach.

We now live in a world in which everyone has heard of AA and knows that it is a fellowship of people who were alcoholic and who have quit drinking. Once people admit to themselves that they are alcoholic, the only excuse to continue drinking, it seems (other than stubbornly wanting to fix it themselves), is the suspicion that life sober in AA would be somehow worse than it is now. In the stories in this book, Renee talks about her fear of life being boring without drugs and alcohol. The refusal of the call, like the call to adventure, can go on day after day, week after week, month after month, and sadly often year after year.

I knew a man who quit drinking and went to AA for about four months one year when his kids were ages six and eight. He went back to drinking for whatever reason and didn't stop again until another sixteen years had passed. That this time in his life and that of his family was lost is a real tragedy. Many of the stories recount years of misery with no effort at recovery. No doubt all of them had their moments when they thought something had to be done, but by the next day, they were back at it again with no further serious thought of changing their behavior. I have heard people tell stories at AA of having first come to AA twenty and thirty years before they finally quit drinking for good.

Eventually, all the storytellers here accepted the call. Renee, Charles, Niall, and Susan all relapsed after their initial efforts at recovery. Fortunately, for Renee and Niall, it was a one-time marijuana relapse. Hawk, Steve, Youngblood, and James did not relapse at all once they were introduced to the twelve step path. In Bill Wilson's case, his acceptance of the call immediately followed a dramatic spiritual experience of an otherworldly nature. He was transported to a mountaintop, where a great spiritual wind blew. Jacob had a dream in which he saw angels climbing up and down a ladder extending to heaven. God stood at the top of the ladder, promising His protection and telling him that he would be the father of a great nation.

The responses of the two men could not have been more different. Bill Wilson knew that he would never drink again because of his vision and wanted to share it with the world so that every alcoholic could recover. Jacob told God that if He kept His promise, then Jacob would let Him be his God and that he would give him a 10 percent commission on his profits. So, it seems that Jacob's acceptance of the call was conditional. Years later, he had a second otherworldly experience that helped him to accept God unconditionally.

Hawk's profound spiritual experience was not immediate. In his third year of sobriety, while "seeking God," he felt connected to God and the universe during a sweat lodge ceremony. He was subsequently taught the sacred pipe ceremony and has prayed in that manner since, sharing the way with a great many people also "seeking God." None of the others in the stories related here shared anything so dramatic, but all were eventually transformed.

To many people at the point of surrender, the gift of AA at first doesn't seem like much of a gift, but at least it is something and more than what they were working with on their own. The gifts offered in these stories, except for that of Hawk, were not of a magical object. Hawk was taught the sacred pipe (*chanupa*) ceremony. For Hawk, as well as all the others, the gift was the twelve step program, the fellowship, the meetings, and sponsorship. For many of the people in our stories, gifts were granted in the form of random people who appeared, offered them a life-changing gift, and then vanished from their lives.

For Niall, it was a couple who drove up to where he was contemplating suicide and commenced to make love in the backseat of their car. He took it as an answer to his prayer to God for a sign telling him to not kill himself. (Bill Wilson's vision also occurred after he asked God for a sign.) For Youngblood, it was a fellow inmate who offered her a release from a long prison term and a man who gave her a ride, a meal, and fellowship when she was released from confinement. For Bill Wilson, it was Father Ed, who appeared when he was at his lowest point and became his spiritual advisor. For Renee, it was her former teacher who appeared to her in a dream when she was in treatment.

I think of these people who come, work a miracle, and then go as angels. A friend of mine was homeless and drunk in Chicago years ago. He went down into a subway station, planning to jump in front of the next train and end it all. As he stood on the platform, a train approaching, what he describes as a "young hippie woman" touched him on the arm and leaned up close to him so she could speak into his ear. "Don't," she said. He didn't, and when the train stopped, she got on. Of course, he never saw her again.

Miracles happen when we least expect them. It pays to be open-minded enough to see them when they occur. Of course, almost everyone on the twelve step pathway of recovery will tell you that a miracle has happened in their lives. They know that a power has entered their lives and made it possible for them to stop destroying themselves, be transformed, and become useful members of society, something they could never have accomplished on their own. What brought this about was a power greater than themselves.

The acceptance of the call to adventure is marked by the completion of the third step. A decision has been made to put oneself in the hands of a higher power. The heroic *quest* can now begin. The attainment of the quest, in my view, is marked by the completion of step 9, as attested in the Ninth Step Promises.

Some of our storytellers more than others talk about how working through the steps played a crucial role in their recovery. Hawk says that working the twelve steps has allowed him to lose the fear that consumed him every day of his life and that he is "able to help others with their recovery, participate in life on life's terms, and feel truly content." He adds, "The promises mentioned after step 9 in the Big Book continue to come true as I work for them each day." They all emphasize that, without being honest with themselves about the roles they played in their own troubles, they would never have stayed in recovery. Charles tells us that he does a weekly tenth step, a weekly self-examination with his sponsor. He continues this practice despite being sober now for thirty-five years. It is a good example of the value of continued practice of the steps. Renee talks about the seriousness with which she approached the fourth and fifth steps after her relapse on marijuana. Clearly, the daily practice of tenth step self-examination is a key to prevent backsliding.

Prayer is mentioned as a valuable element in their recovery tool kit by many of our storytellers. Bill Wilson prayed every day, even though he never decided exactly what to think about who or what God was. He talked in such terms as the spirit of the universe, and Christ seemed to be very important to him. Later in his recovery, he took instruction in the Catholic faith but never converted.

Renee talks about the wall she built up between herself and God. As a sixth-grader, she believed God had punished her for smoking marijuana by giving her scarlet fever. She says the wall started to crumble in treatment when a nurse refused to give her a sleeping pill and suggested that she pray instead. She reluctantly tried it, and after a good night's sleep, she found herself starting to be willing to listen when people were advising her to try prayer. It was just around that time when her former teacher visited her in a dream telling her she could be successful if she made the effort. A few months later, when her daughter was hospitalized with a brain tumor, Renee found herself in the hospital chapel making what she considers to be her first sincere prayer, asking God to watch over her little girl.

Hawk says he was desperate to find a higher power because the program taught that one was necessary for recovery. In his search, he attended a spiritual renewal retreat and was introduced to a sweat lodge ceremony. Here he had a spiritual experience, found his higher power, and learned the way to pray that was right for him. He has traveled the Red Road ever since.

Niall writes about the night he planned suicide but stopped to "have one last talk with God." He asked for a sign not to kill himself. Shortly thereafter, a car pulled up, and a couple made love in the backseat. Niall always has believed that God has a sense of humor, so clearly this was his sign. He talks about how his upbringing and experiences in Catholic school just made God seem frightening. After more than thirty years in AA, Niall says that his relationship with God is the most important thing in his life.

Steve observes that the program suggests "seeking God," so that is what he has done, although he does not believe he has found God. His level of willingness to do what is suggested is exemplified by the fact that, every morning, as suggested by his sponsor more than thirty years ago, he gets on his knees and prays—this even though he considers himself to be an atheist. While this may not make sense to some people, it makes sense to him as willingness to do what is suggested and not worry about the reason or the result. One beneficial result is that he has not had a drink in more than thirty-four years.

Charles says that trusting in God has been of great benefit on his journey. Youngblood talks with some rough language about what she used to think about God while she was living her addicted life. While in jail facing serious prison time, she made what she refers to as her "foxhole prayer," telling God that if He got her out of there, then she would do whatever He wanted her to do. She did get out, and although not perfectly, she has held up her side of the bargain. James credits God for directing his path and says he trusts that God will continue to guide him.

It is of no use to travel the heroic path and attain the quest unless the treasure is brought back to the kingdom for the good of others. All our storytellers emphasize the importance of the fellowship to their ongoing well-being. And they, to a greater or lesser degree, stress the value of connecting with themselves and others on a spiritual level. This includes working with others, whether as a sponsor or a speaker at a meeting or simply answering the phone when it rings.

James and Youngblood have become treatment professionals as part of their commitment to serving other addicts in need. Renee talks about how she was able to reach out to a woman she met at an AA meeting who, like Renee, had lost her husband. This story is instructive in another way. The day after her husband died, this woman thought it was important enough to go to an AA meeting. Neither Hawk nor Susan mentions it in their stories, but I am aware that they both went back to where they were treated and served as volunteers, working with the newcomers, and testifying to the success of the program in their lives.

Charles tells us, "Sharing my experience with other alcoholics and particularly newcomers has been the source of a particularly strong sense of God's presence and has given me tremendous satisfaction." He also says, "Sharing the common demons of fear, doubt, and insecurity on a one-to-one basis seems to strengthen my God connection, and serenity usually rapidly follows."

Steve is very active in service work, at times going way out of his way to help someone in need. He says,

> An essential part of my quest for sobriety includes service, which, for me, mostly takes the form of service in AA. This includes working with newcomers, participating in a home group, sponsoring people, speaking when asked, being present and participating in meetings, and being available any time there is any other alcoholic who needs help. The foundation of the AA program is that one alcoholic helps another, and that service helps the first stay sober.

All the people in these stories attained their quest of sobriety. They accomplished something that, unaided, they never could have made happen in their lives. In the process of achieving their quest, each discovered that they had become different people, able to do, say, or accomplish things that heretofore would have been impossible. They had embarked, unwittingly, on an interior journey of self-discovery that eventuated, remarkably, in self-love. They have not become saints, but they have all been transformed. Now they realize that the journey never ends, that each day is another day they are called on to be heroic, self-aware, and God-aware and to do the next right thing. Their journey is one of spiritual development and growth.

Of all the stories told here, I think the person who made the least commitment to spiritual growth is Jacob. We hear nothing of him making amends to his father for the deception. He has learned nothing about not showing favoritism to certain children. He sent his son Joseph to "check up" on his brothers, giving little regard to how they might feel about it or what they might do. There is little in the story to suggest he achieved a sense of inner peace or spiritual fulfillment. However, we need to cut him some slack because he didn't have the Bible to rely on or the twelve steps to follow. He didn't have a program. Even though he had remarkable spiritual experiences, the effect was not what it might have been.

The other stories in this book share the commonality of people who are immensely grateful for who they have become and for being released from the diabolical trap of active addiction. All speak of helping others on their own heroic journeys of recovery. Youngblood and James have made working with others their life's work.

While the storytellers come from different backgrounds, they wind up at the same place. Three people talk about being raised Catholic. Two say they were raised in a traditional Jewish home. Two were raised Baptist. One clearly had no religion in the home. Two of them were abused. Two were impoverished as children. None came from a wealthy family.

One got sober at age twenty-one, and one got sober at age seventy-two. Four of the group have been continuously sober for more than thirty years. At the other extreme, the kid, Youngblood, and the old gal, Susan, have five years of sobriety. One woman is openly gay. One storyteller is African American but didn't mention this in the story. All of them have found themselves able to help others when the need arises. This is most apparent in Renee's story. Not long after she came home from treatment, her daughter had to have surgery for a brain tumor. That Renee was able to remain sober and take care of her daughter was another miracle.

The people who shared their personal stories in this book are typical of those whom you might meet at an AA meeting. I thank them for their generosity. James told me that, if it would help someone, he would do it. I had the story a few days later. If there is anything remarkable about this small group of people, it is that they are so typical. Their similarities are so much greater than their differences.

While the heroic quest is an epic struggle of overcoming one's shadow, demons, dark side, or however one wants to think about it, these stories tell of an even more heroic and epic journey: of being transformed and dealing with the rest of one's life, one day at a time, with courage, acceptance, compassion, and serenity. One does not recover from an addiction and then live an unchallenged life. The twelve steps continue to provide the needed guidance to confront whatever life puts in front of the hero.

What is it about the twelve step program that provides an ongoing GPS for life in recovery? The most important element, I believe, comes with the first word of the first step: *we.* Addiction is a lonely illness. Not only do addicts feel lost and abandoned, but at some level, they believe that they deserve such desertion by others. Talking with those who have walked into their very first twelve step group, we hear over and over that there was a sense of camaraderie and fellowship that had great appeal. Indeed, the alcoholic has arrived in a fellowship where there is no judgment or condemnation for having attained such an admittedly defeated condition.

In Renee's story, she comments that she was "met with open arms." And it is one thing to get to an AA meeting and quite another to want to keep coming back. Steve tells us, "Another inducement to continue with AA attendance was the social aspect because I had become pretty socially isolated, and I enjoyed the company of the people at AA."

The program can be quite bewildering for many, even for such well-educated people as Charles. Charles reports, "I was finally able to comprehend the first step with the love of the program of Alcoholics Anonymous and the help of a patient sponsor." The "love of the program of Alcoholics Anonymous" Charles refers to, of course, is the people in Alcoholics Anonymous. And Susan tells us that she "cherishes the friendships she has made."

For those who have not had the experience, it is hard to imagine how radically different and gratifying it is to find that, for the same reasons alcoholics were loathed and condemned, they are greeted with love and good humor by the fellowship. "I'm Niall, or I'm Renee, or I'm Charles, and I'm an alcoholic" is a positive statement, an affirmation that the individual has embarked on and accepted a new way of life. The newcomer has been greeted with the promise "You don't have to hate yourself; you can do better with your life. We have done so with our lives, and we will show you how it is done." In such a situation, surrender can be accompanied by great relief.

This promise is believable because of the smiling faces the newcomers see and their own ongoing success, and it is validated by the results they can see in others. At first, they must take the word of the AA members that they were as bad off, but in time, the newcomers not only can experience the changes themselves but also can observe change in others who come into the program in the days, weeks, and months after their own arrival. In time, the newcomers see the value of getting out of their own way in life's journey and deciding each day to put God's will first.

This will mean different things to different people. This is as it should be because each of us is a unique individual who has a unique relationship with a higher power. As time goes on, it becomes more apparent that this commitment needs to be renewed each day. There is no heroic journey that allows for a time-out on the way. People who slip away from good recovery habits leave the door wide open for old habits of thinking, especially self-centeredness, to take control. So ongoing self-awareness and God-awareness are indispensable guides on the journey of life.

It is interesting to see the frequent use by our storytellers of the words *journey* and *quest*. It is as though they intuitively know that their experiences recapitulate the archetypal quest for wholeness and the archetypal journey that one must travel on the way. Renee says that, after she told her story at an AA meeting in her second year of sobriety to a group that included many newcomers, she was "filled with that wondrous calm and gratitude that continues to embrace me at different times in my journey." And she adds at the end of her story, "The journey continues to be challenging at times, it never gets boring, and I'm forever grateful for the divine intervention that led me to our life-changing fellowship." Remember that her fear had been that a life without drugs and alcohol would be boring.

Niall refers to his journey when he says, "The toughest part of my journey was probably the first twenty-five years of my sobriety." This thought could be very discouraging to a newcomer. Really? Twenty-five more bad years? The truth is that he is referring to a lot of continued struggles with his feelings during a time in which, for the most part, he enjoyed his life. And he stayed sober. Furthermore, he adds that a particularly difficult time for him was "what I needed to move forward on my recovery journey."

Steve talks about his "quest for sobriety." Charles says, "This journey in sobriety has given me my life back." Youngblood says that she was "walked through this journey by people who swore they understood." She adds that she has "learned to navigate" her feelings and situations. Again, she states that the "most important gift that has been bestowed upon me as a result of my sobriety and my journey is the ability to truly impact others' lives." It seems that she is equating her sobriety with her journey. They are inseparable.

Susan refers to her journey when she says, "So that's my story, and my journey continues. I can't say I'm grateful I am an alcoholic, but I can say that I never want to go back to drinking. And I am grateful that there are all these tools to help me on my journey." James talks about his "own journey of helping addicted men recover and find their own way." Interestingly, he says that what he can do is be of assistance, but ultimately, each person must live their own life and "find their own way." He adds that he can "look forward to experiencing what God has in store for me on this incredible journey."

Those on the heroic journey will continue to be challenged by life, at times with painful circumstances to confront. Shortly after treatment, Renee's younger daughter had surgery for a malignant brain tumor. Although the tumor was removed and she was cured, she was left with some paralysis. Also, during her first year of recovery, her brother died from AIDS, and her first husband petitioned the Catholic Church for an annulment of their marriage. Several years later, her second husband died of cancer.

Bill Wilson suffered severe bouts of depression that were at times incapacitating. After Jacob's transformation at the River Jabbok, he endured the death of his wife; the disappearance of his son; the rape of his daughter; the disgrace of his son's slaughtering the people of Shechem in retaliation; the arrest of his youngest son, Benjamin, in Egypt; and the forced relocation to Egypt because of famine. Niall was divorced and prevented from having contact with his son for several years. He had a serious dirt-bike accident that incapacitated him for a long time and left him with chronic pain. He came too close to suicide. His relationships with his siblings seem to be irreparably damaged.

Life is challenging, and the fact that the heroes have returned to the kingdom spiritually transformed doesn't immunize them from the same kinds of stresses and losses that everyone else must face. What has changed is the heroes are now at a place where life can be accepted on life's terms. By practicing the twelve steps every day, the heroes maintain balance and a sense of peacefulness beyond their comprehension prior to embarking on the heroic journey.

Everyone has their own story to tell. All the writers of the stories in this book thanked me for the opportunity to tell their stories here. I did no cherry-picking when I looked for storytellers. In my own circle of friends and acquaintances, I could have asked many others, and the result would have been the same. They would have been eager to share, and what they shared would have been as instructive as the stories here. I want every reader of this book to know that they have a journey to take and a story to tell. I wish you all safe travels on the road to recovery.

Chapter Ten

Workbook

Understanding Your Own Heroic Journey of Recovery

In this book, I use the heroic journey as a means of understanding and overcoming the difficulties we have encountered in our own lives. For many, these difficulties manifested as a life-destroying addiction that could not be overcome unaided. This chapter will help you think through what this means in your own life. If addiction was not applicable to you, then adapt the questions to your situation. Using paper or electronically, use the following questions to stimulate your thinking, and write down your answers. There are no wrong answers. This is your search for your own truth.

What does being heroic mean to you?

Some famous people are often thought of as heroic, such as George Washington, Abraham Lincoln, Nelson Mandela, Jackie Robinson, Harriet Tubman, Mother Teresa, and Mohandas Gandhi. List three historic figures whom you see as heroic and explain why you think they are heroes. List three heroic people whom you know from your own life. Why do you think they are heroic?

Give some examples of how your addiction was making your life unmanageable.

Give some examples of what you tried to overcome your addiction.

In the classical hero's tale, the hero receives a call to adventure. In the case of addiction, this usually comes from an incident that calls attention to the uncontrolled drinking or other addictive behavior and its consequences. This is typically followed by a refusal of the call or a wish to refuse. Give some examples of times that you were confronted with the need to change your behavior but failed to do so.

For people in recovery, the day comes when they have reached what the Big Book calls the "turning point." This is the day they know they will never stop what they are doing on their own and they realize they need outside help. Have you reached a turning point? Write about how this happened and how it was different from all the other times you failed to surrender.

Some people relapse after a prolonged period of abstinence and eventually reenter the recovery path. If this is your case, then there was a second or possibly even more "turning points." Write about this.

The hero is promised that he will not be alone on the quest, that he or she will receive powers that will allow them to accomplish what could not have otherwise been done. On your journey, what aid or powers have been given to you? These powers could be God, a sponsor, the twelve steps, or something else. What outside powers have you received, and how did they help you on your journey?

I talk about the heroic journey as two journeys in one. The first journey is the adventure of abstaining from our addiction while living in the same world in which we could never abstain before. Talk about what this journey was like for you. What stresses did you navigate? What temptations did you overcome? How did you succeed? What were the first few days, weeks, and months like?

Some heroes descend into hell on their journeys, either figuratively or literally. Jonah spent three days in the belly of a whale. Saint Paul was incarcerated many times. Nelson Mandela was a political prisoner for twenty-seven years. Can you identify times when you descended into your own personal hell? If so, write about these times, what they were like, and how you survived. Did you receive help from a power greater than yourself?

The second journey is that of venturing inward and looking honestly and fearlessly at yourself. This requires courage. What does being courageous mean to you? When in your life have you been courageous? If you have completed your fourth step, then write about how you found the courage to do this step.

The Big Book talks about ego and playing God. It discusses the need for ego deflation at depth. Write what your understanding is about how you played God. What do you understand about your inflated ego? Give examples.

Paradoxically, with the inflated egos, alcoholics also recognize that they are extremely insecure and suffer from low self-esteem: "the ego-maniac with the inferiority complex." Write your own thoughts about yourself that reflected your poor self-esteem.

A personality trait emphasized in the Big Book and acquired as the result of traveling on the heroic journey is humility. Bill Wilson talks about this, as well, in *Twelve Steps and Twelve Traditions*, especially in chapter 7. He wrote about it extensively in his Grapevine articles. What does humility mean to you? Do you see it as a desirable trait for you to develop? Can you see the relationship between humility and ego deflation at depth? Give some examples of how you know you have become more humble. Give some examples of how you know that you have room to grow along these lines.

A time comes in recovery when the heroes realize that something is really different. They have changed. The obsession has been removed. This is the attainment of the quest, but the journey is not yet over. As pointed out in chapter 7, while the dragon has been slain, it retains the capacity to put its severed head back on its shoulders and eat the hero alive. We may slowly become aware of having been transformed as we travel the heroic path of recovery, but such a realization can be fully identified after completion of the ninth step. In the Big Book, certain statements are made about the changes that have taken place by this time. These statements are generally referred to in the program as the Ninth Step Promises. I like to think of these promises as arrival stations on the heroic journey.

The first of these promises is that we will experience a "new freedom and a new happiness."[1] The emphasis is on the word *new*. Can you say this about yourself? If so, talk about what your new freedom and new happiness is like and what it means to you. Do you believe it came about as the result of the efforts made on your journey thus far? If so, why do you believe this?

The second promise is "We will not regret the past nor wish to shut the door on it."[2] What regrets, if any, do you still have about the past? Is there remaining guilt or shame? If so, does this mean that you are not doing the program right? Are you willing to be patient on your heroic journey? In a way, holding onto guilt and shame reflects the old ego, and false pride is still present. Do you see this? This is not a condemna-tion. It simply describes what normally happens. It is important to be entirely willing to let this go, or it can become a seed for an eventual relapse. Does this make sense to you? Write about why this may be true for you. I think not regretting the past is an ideal that not everyone can fully attain. If you are not yet there, then try to accept the reality that you are indeed on a journey. Stay the course, and things will improve.

The third promise says, "We will comprehend the word serenity and we will know peace."[3] In what way is this true for you? Do you have more times of calm in your life? Do you get as worked up in times of stress? If so, can you calm down faster than you used to? What does the word *serenity* mean to you? Have you gained skills in which you can become serene? What are these skills? Very likely, they work better and last longer than drug use, and they don't cause hangovers or demand more drinks or drugs. Can you write about how your addiction prevented you from being serene?

The fourth promise says, "No matter how far down the scale we have gone, we will see how our experience can benefit others."[4] How far down the scale did you go? In AA, people talk about hitting bottom, but it seems that the degree of bottoms vary. We talk about "low-bottom" and "high-bottom" alcoholics. Most probably fall in the middle. Where do you see yourself? If you have suffered greatly or caused others to suffer greatly because of your addiction and addictive behaviors, can you forgive yourself? Do you believe that by your recovery you can benefit others? If so, in what ways can you do so?

The fifth promise says, "That feeling of uselessness and self-pity will disappear."[5] Has this come true or started to for you? Did you feel useless? Has this changed? Write about in what ways this has improved. Undoubtedly you felt sorry for yourself. All addicts do. Write the reasons you told yourself that life wasn't fair, that you had gotten a raw deal, that your life was a terrible one. Bill put the idea of feeling useless and having self-pity in the same sentence. Why do you think he did that?

The next promise states, "We will lose interest in selfish things and gain interest in our fellows." The following promise says, "Self-seeking will slip away."[6] In what ways do you see that you were self-absorbed while in active addiction? In what ways did you neglect the needs of other people in your life? Give some examples of how this has changed. Give some examples that show you still have room to grow.

Promise 8 (depending on how you count, of course) says, "Our whole attitude and outlook upon life will change."[7] Write about what your attitude was before you embarked on the heroic journey of recovery. How positive or negative was your outlook on life? What is your attitude about yourself, and what is your outlook on life now? How has your own heroism in taking this journey brought about this change? How much comes from a power greater than yourself?

The next promise states, "Fear of people and of economic insecurity will leave us."[8] (This is really two promises, but the way they relate to each other is through fear.) Write about your fear of people, both before and during your addiction. Has this changed? Write about what is better, and if you still have some fears of people, then write about this as well. There is a difference between economic insecurity and the *fear* of economic insecurity. Without making too fine a point of this, write about your own economic insecurity. Has this improved? It usually does simply because, in recovery, people are more employable, but individual situations vary. To what degree does your economic insecurity or fear of it disturb your serenity?

Fear of economic insecurity is related to a larger problem, which is uncertainty in life. One of the great challenges in life is dealing with uncertainty. Traveling the heroic journey makes uncertainty easier to cope with. Do you see how uncertainty has troubled you in your life? If you can, write about how fears and uncertainty fueled your addiction. Do you see how the twelve step path of recovery offers tools to help you to deal with uncertainty? Write about this.

The next promise (call it promise 11) says, "We will intuitively know how to handle situations which used to baffle us."[9] Have you experienced this yet? Is this not a great confidence boost and gratitude shot when it happens? Give some examples, if you can, of this promise coming true in your life.

The twelfth promise states, "We will suddenly realize that God is doing for us what we could not do for ourselves."[10] Has this realization come to you yet? If so, write about how and when this happened. This promise clearly says that we know that we could never have brought about the improvement in our lives without the assistance of a higher power. We can only know this if we have both had the improvement and can see it from the position of a humbled ego. The feeling that arises within us at this point of realization is gratitude. Write about the ways that you feel grateful for the life you have today.

By this time, the hero is starting to realize that there is no end to his or her journey in this lifetime. The gains made can only be maintained by continued travel. This travel is a must, both in the daily life of action, as well as in the interior journey of self-knowledge and spiritual development. Step 10 calls for continued self-awareness and self-evaluation, as well as for prompt admission if an old defect of character shows up. This self-evaluation is best accomplished if the hero has a plan in place and acts on it daily. Do you have a plan for step 10? If so, what is your plan? Write it out now. Do you think it is adequate? Are you accountable to anyone for carrying it out? This is a place where a sponsor can be valuable.

Do you have a sponsor? If not, why? What ego factors have prevented you from having and using a sponsor? Remember, the hero is promised aid on the journey, and in the case of twelve step recovery, the sponsor is an important, even vital, element in the process. If you do have a sponsor, how do you use them? How often do you meet or talk? Do you talk about problems encountered on the journey or just chitchat? How honest can you be with your sponsor? Have you ever changed sponsors? If so, for what reason? Not that there is anything wrong with changing, per se. Sometimes on a new leg of the journey, you need someone who has something new and different to offer you. The important thing is to be honest with yourself. Remember also that people in recovery find that relationships are among the most difficult things to deal with, and sponsorship relationships can be challenging, as well. Can you write about challenges you have had, either with your sponsor or when sponsoring others?

I mention the risk of relapse and liken it to the reawakening of the sleeping dragon, the release of the dragon from the place within us where it was incapacitated. I just described how self-awareness can help to keep us safe from such a disaster. The other kind of awareness that is necessary to maintain daily is God awareness. Call it spiritual awareness if this term is more suitable for you. This is where we rely on and use the eleventh step.

Do you pray? If so, do you pray every day? Do you have a special time of day when you pray? Do you use specific prayers, such as the Serenity Prayer? Do you have specific prayers from your own religious practice? Some people talk to God in their own words and find this the most effective form of prayer for themselves. Do you talk to God? Write about how you think you could improve your prayer life. Write about how you believe prayer has benefited you on your journey.

Often when people pray, they ask God for something. The eleventh step says to ask only for God's will for us and the power to carry it out. Do you agree that this is all you can request of God? Whether you agree with this suggestion or not, write out your thoughts about it. Many people when they arrive at the start of their heroic journeys have lost their faith and belief in God. Some people, as a result of the journey, come to either a renewed or a newly found belief in God. Has this happened for you? If so, write about it.

Meditation is an ancient practice with proven benefits in many aspects of life that are crucial for recovery. For example, it will improve one's conscious contact with a higher power, the stated purpose of the step. Some people say that prayer is talking to God and meditation is listening to God. Does this idea work for you? Do you meditate? If so, write about your meditation practice and in what way you believe that it benefits you. If not, what are your barriers to meditation? Write about listening to God if you have had this experience. If you have experienced enhanced contact with your higher power through meditation, write about this experience and how it has furthered the maintenance of your spiritual condition.

A common theme that guides us on our journey is that of willingness. Write about how your unwillingness has caused you trouble on your journey. Write about how you benefited when you became willing.

The Big Book uses the expressions *spiritual experience* and *spiritual awakening*. The goal of the inward component of the heroic journey is the union with the spirit of the universe, God, or whatever term works best for you. The twelfth step starts by stating, "Having had a spiritual awakening as the result of these steps."[11] Do you believe that you have had a spiritual awakening? What does or would it mean to you to have a spiritual awakening? If you have had a spiritual awakening, have there been times when you seem to have lost it? If so, why do you think this happened? What did you do to reinvigorate your spiritual life?

The twelfth step goes on to say, "We tried to carry this message to alcoholics."[12] The heroes in the classical heroic-journey format, after they have their adventures, bring something of immense value back to their home communities as the final step. This boon or treasure relieves the suffering of their fellows. Indeed, in a way this is the most important function of a hero. It can't just be about the hero as an isolated person.

What have you done to carry the message to other alcoholics (or whichever term is appropriate to your situation)? Do you sponsor others? Do you volunteer for other kinds of service work? Do you approach newcomers at meetings? Write about how working with others has benefited you on your journey of recovery. Why is your recovery not just important to you?

The last suggestion of step 12 is to "practice these principles in all our affairs."[13] In AA, this means "do the next right thing." Many people are devoted to helping others as part of this step and give much less attention to practicing these principles in all their affairs. Is that the case with you? Sometimes it is not entirely clear what the next right thing to do is. How do you handle these situations? Reasonable options would be to think, rely on past experiences, ask your sponsor, pray, or get expert guidance. Sometimes, perhaps often, doing nothing is the best choice in any given moment. Have you delayed making a decision and found things working out for the best without your intervention? While people are hesitant to do the next right thing because of uncertainty, often the problem is fear. Can you think of when you hesitated to do what was right because of fear?

An aspect of "all our affairs" that deserves specific attention is our relationships. A good practice is to be mindful of how we treat the other people we encounter each day. Write about how you interact with others. Are you compassionate, kind, respectful, helpful, considerate, loving, and honest? Or do you show frustration, impatience, or anger or try to control others? Write about where your daily practice of your personal affairs is something you feel good about. Be specific. And write about where you could have done better and need improvement.

I hope and pray that this series of exercises is beneficial to each of you on your heroic journey of recovery. I hope all of you come to believe and feel that you are worthy of being loved. I hope that you can properly give yourselves credit for the incredible bravery it has taken to accept the challenge that life has offered you. And I hope that you realize the importance of sharing what you have gained with others. I do wish you all continued success and joy as you travel the "Road of Happy Destiny."

Notes

INTRODUCTION

1. Joseph Campbell, *The Power of Myth* (Anchor Books, 1991), 57.
2. *Alcoholics Anonymous: The Story of How Many Thousands of Men and Women Have Recovered from Alcoholism*, 4th ed. (Alcoholics Anonymous World Services, 2001), 55.
3. Ibid., 47.
4. Ibid., 55.

JACOB'S STORY

1. Gen. 28:10–15. As in all other translations from the Bible quoted in this book, unless I quote other authors who incorporate a different translation, I use the New International Version (NIV).
2. Gen. 27:22.
3. Gen. 29:17.
4. Gen. 32:24–30.

CHAPTER ONE

1. Michael Murphy, *Golf in the Kingdom* (Penguin Random House, 2022).
2. *Alcoholics Anonymous: The Story of How Many Thousands of Men and Women Recovered from Alcoholism*, 4th ed. (Alcoholics Anonymous World Services, 2001), 55.

CHAPTER TWO

1. Robert Thomsen, *Bill W.* (Harper and Row, 1975), 15.
2. Ibid., 36.
3. Ibid., 96.
4. Ibid., 147.
5. Ibid., 191.
6. Ibid., 207.
7. Ibid., 216.
8. Ibid., 233.
9. Ibid., 234.
10. Ibid., 243.
11. Ibid., 288.
12. Ernest Kurtz, *Not-God: A History of Alcoholics Anonymous* (Hazelden, 1991), 98–99.
13. Thomsen, *Bill W.*, 270.
14. William H. Schaberg, *Writing "The Big Book": The Creation of A.A* (Central Recovery Press, 2019), 87.
15. Ibid., 94.
16. Ibid., 124.
17. Ibid., 563.
18. Kurtz, *Not-God*, 75.
19. Dick B., *The Oxford Group and Alcoholics Anonymous: A Design for Living That Works* (Paradise Research, 1998), 146.
20. Schaberg, *Writing "The Big Book,"* 556.
21. Ibid., 596.
22. Ibid., 193.
23. John L., "Washingtonian Forebears of Alcoholics Anonymous," *AA Agnostica* (blog), July 15, 2012, https://aaagnostica.org/2012/07/15/washingtonian-forbears-of-alcoholics-anonymous/.
24. *Twelve Steps and Twelve Traditions* (Alcoholics Anonymous, 1953), 140.
25. Bill W., *Alcoholics Anonymous Comes of Age: A Brief History of AA* (Alcoholics Anonymous, 1957), 223–28.
26. *"Pass It On": Bill Wilson and How the AA Message Reached the World* (Alcoholics Anonymous, 1984), 368; "*Time* 100 Persons of the Century," *Time*, June 14, 1999, https://content.time.com/time/magazine/article/0,9171,26473,00.html.

CHAPTER THREE

1. American Psychiatric Association, *Diagnostic and Statistical Manual of Mental Disorders, Fifth Edition, Text Revision, DSM-5—TR* (American Psychiatric Association, 2022).

2. American Society of Addictive Medicine, "Definition of Addiction," updated September 15, 2019, https://www.asam.org/quality-care/definition-of-addiction.

3. "The Doctor's Opinion," in *Alcoholics Anonymous: The Story of How Many Thousands of Men and Women Recovered from Alcoholism*, 4th ed., xxv–xxxii (Alcoholics Anonymous World Services, 2001).

RENEE'S STORY

1. "The Doctor's Opinion," in *Alcoholics Anonymous: The Story of How Many Thousands of Men and Women Recovered from Alcoholism*, 4th ed., xxv–xxxii (Alcoholics Anonymous World Services, 2001).

2. *Alcoholics Anonymous: The Story of How Many Thousands of Men and Women Recovered from Alcoholism*, 4th ed. (Alcoholics Anonymous World Services, 2001), 22.

3. *Twelve Steps and Twelve Traditions* (Alcoholics Anonymous, 1957).

CHAPTER FOUR

1. *Alcoholics Anonymous*, 59.

2. Bill W., *Alcoholics Anonymous Comes of Age: A Brief History of A.A.* (Alcoholics Anonymous, 1957), 199.

3. Quoted in Julia Cameron, *The Artist's Way: A Spiritual Path to Higher Creativity* (Jeremy P. Tarcher/Putnam, 1992), 171.

4. William James, *The Varieties of Religious Experience: A Study in Human Nature* (Random House Modern Library, 1902), 207, quoted in Ernest Kurtz, *Not-God: A History of Alcoholics Anonymous* (Hazelden, 1991), 21.

5. Chuck C., *A New Pair of Glasses* (New Look, 1984), 126.

6. Quoted in Kurtz, *Not-God*, 61.

7. Eckhart Tolle, *The Power of Now: A Guide to Spiritual Enlightenment* (New World Library, 1999), 218.

8. *Alcoholics Anonymous*, 59.

9. *Alcoholics Anonymous: The Story of How Many Thousands of Men and Women Recovered from Alcoholism*, 4th ed. (Alcoholics Anonymous World Services, 2001), 45.

10. Gabriel Marcel, *Homo Viator: Introduction to the Metaphysics of Hope* (St. Augustine's Press, 2010), 5.

11. Milton Steinberg, *Basic Judaism* (New York: Harcourt, Brace, 1947), 39–40.

12. Aldous Huxley, *The Perennial Philosophy* (Harper Perennial Modern Classics, 2004), 25.

13. Robert Thomsen, *Bill W.* (Harper and Row, 1975), 367.

14. *Alcoholics Anonymous*, 47, emphasis mine.

15. Peter J. Gomes, introduction to Paul Tillich, *The Courage to Be*, 2nd ed. (Yale University Press, 2000), xxiii.

16. *Alcoholics Anonymous*, 59.

17. Quoted in Cameron, *Artist's Way*, 199.

18. Ibid., 193.

19. James, *Varieties of Religious Experience*, 207.

20. Bill W., *Alcoholics Anonymous Comes of Age*, 247–48.

21. Chuck C., *New Pair of Glasses*, 24.

22. Bill W., *The Language of the Heart: Bill W.'s Grapevine Writings* (AA Grapevine, 1988), 245–46.

23. Kurtz, *Not-God*, 183.

24. Sigmund Freud, *On Narcissism* (1914).

25. Dick B., *The Oxford Group and Alcoholics Anonymous: A Design for Living That Works* (Paradise Research, 1998), 78.

26. Ibid., 170.

27. Patrick Carnes, *A Gentle Path through the Twelve Steps* (Hazelden, 2012).

CHAPTER FIVE

1. *Alcoholics Anonymous*, 59.

2. Murray Stein, *Jung's Map of the Soul* (Open Court, 1998), 106.

3. Romans 7:18–19.

4. Mark M. Mattison, trans., "The Gospel of Thomas: A Public Domain Translation," accessed June 13, 2023, https://www.academia.edu/15107954/The_Gospel_of_Thomas_A_Public_Domain_Translation.

5. Stein, *Jung's Map*, 122.

6. *Alcoholics Anonymous*, 59.

7. Vernon J. Bourke, *Augustine's Quest for Wisdom: Life and Philosophy of the Bishop of Hippo* (Bruce, 1945), 148.

8. *Alcoholics Anonymous: The Story of How Many Thousands of Men and Women Recovered from Alcoholism*, 4th ed. (Alcoholics Anonymous World Services, 2001), 58.

9. Ibid., 59.

10. Ibid., 75.

11. *Twelve Steps and Twelve Traditions* (Alcoholics Anonymous, 1953), 57.

CHAPTER SIX

1. *Alcoholics Anonymous*, 59.

2. *Twelve Steps and Twelve Traditions* (Alcoholics Anonymous, 1953), 69.

3. *Alcoholics Anonymous*, 59.

4. Stephanie S. Covington, *A Woman's Way through the Twelve Steps* (Hazelden, 1994), 110.

5. Francis K. Nemeck and Marie T. Coombs, *O Blessed Night! Recovering from Addiction, Codependency, and Attachment Based on the Insights of St. John of the Cross and Pierre Teilhard de Chardin* (Alba House, 1991), 77.

6. John 15:1–2.

7. *Twelve Steps and Twelve Traditions*, 70.

8. Ernest Kurtz, *Not-God: A History of Alcoholics Anonymous* (Hazelden, 1991), 183.

9. Ibid., 192.

10. Ibid., 195.

11. Martin Buber, *Hasidism and Modern Man* (Humanities Press International, 1958), 104–5.

12. Quoted in Rabbi Edwin Goldberg, Rabbi Janet Marder, Rabbi Sheldon Marder, and Rabbi Leon Morris, eds., *Mishkan HaNefesh: Yom Kippur* (Central Conference of American Rabbis, 2015), 407.

13. Quoted in ibid., 542.

CHAPTER SEVEN

1. *Alcoholics Anonymous*, 59.

2. O. Hobart Mowrer, "Small Groups in Historical Perspective," in *Explorations in Self-Help and Mutual Aid*, ed. Leonard D. Borman (Center for Urban Studies, Northwestern University, 1974), 47.

3. Paul Tillich, *The Courage to Be* (Yale University Press, 1952), 41.

4. Dag Hammarskjöld, *Markings*, trans. Leif Sjöberg and W. H. Auden (Vintage Books, 2006), 124.

5. Jerry Hirschfield, *The Twelve Steps for Everyone . . . Who Really Wants Them* (Hazelden, 1990), 73.

6. *Twelve Steps and Twelve Traditions* (Alcoholics Anonymous, 1953), 82.

7. *Alcoholics Anonymous*, 59.

8. *Alcoholics Anonymous: The Story of How Many Thousands of Men and Women Recovered from Alcoholism*, 4th ed. (Alcoholics Anonymous World Services, 2001), 83–84.

9. *Alcoholics Anonymous*, 83.

10. Ibid., 83.

11. *Alcoholics Anonymous: The Story of How Many Thousands of Men and Women Recovered from Alcoholism*, 4th ed. (Alcoholics Anonymous World Services, 2001), 63.

12. Acts 20:35.

13. *Alcoholics Anonymous*, 83.

14. *Ibid.*, 86.

15. Ibid., 83–84.

16. Bill Pittman, *Stepping Stones to Recovery* (Glen Abbey Books, 1988), 87.

17. Emmet Fox, *Sermon on the Mount: The Key to Success in Life* (HarperSanFrancisco, 1934), 42.

18. *Alcoholics Anonymous*, 84.

19. Ibid., 84.

20. Ibid., 84.

21. Ibid., 84.

22. Howard Thurman, *Meditations of the Heart* (Beacon Press, 1981), 79.

23. *Alcoholics Anonymous*, 84.

CHAPTER EIGHT

1. *Alcoholics Anonymous*, 59.

2. Bill W., *The Language of the Heart: Bill W.'s Grapevine Writings* (AA Grapevine, 1988), 239.

3. Thich Nhat Hanh, *Living Buddha, Living Christ* (Riverhead Books, 1995), 23.

4. Ibid., 19.

5. Jon Kabat-Zinn, *Full Catastrophe Living: Using the Wisdom of Your Body and Mind to Face Stress, Pain, and Illness* (Delacorte Press, 1990), 216–17.

6. Ibid., 216.

7. Stephanie Covington, *A Woman's Way through the Twelve Steps* (Hazelden, 1994), 157.

8. Jerry Hirschfield, *The Twelve Steps for Everyone . . . Who Really Wants Them* (Hazelden, 1990), 86.

9. *Alcoholics Anonymous*, 59.

10. Martin Buber, *Hasidism and Modern Man* (Humanities Press International, 1958), 192.

11. Abraham J. Twerski, *The Spiritual Self: Reflections on Recovery and God* (Hazelden, 2000), 106.

12. Ibid., 108.

13. Quoted in Helen Smith Shoemaker, *I Stand by the Door: The Life of Sam Shoemaker* (Word Books, 1967), 140.

14. *Twelve Steps and Twelve Traditions* (Alcoholics Anonymous, 1953), 98.

15. Job 23:3–4.

16. Harold S. Kushner, *When Bad Things Happen to Good People* (Avon Books, 1981), 10.

17. Ibid., 85.

18. Bill W., *Language of the Heart*, 271.

19. Covington, *Woman's Way*, 210.

20. William L. White, *Slaying the Dragon: The History of Addiction Treatment and Recovery in America* (Chestnut Health Systems/Lighthouse Institute, 2014), 531.

21. *Alcoholics Anonymous*, 84.

22. Emmet Fox, *The Sermon on the Mount: The Key to Success in Life* (HarperSanFrancisco, 1934), 118.

23. Ecclesiastes 3:10–11; Abraham Joshua Heschel, *God in Search of Man: A Philosophy of Judaism* (Farrar, Straus, and Giroux, 1955), 54.

24. Heschel, *God in Search*, 54.

25. Job 32:13.

26. Arthur S. Peake, "Job's Victory," in *The Dimensions of Job: A Study and Selected Readings*, ed. Nahum N. Glatzer (Wipf and Stock, 2002), 204.

27. H. H. Rowley, "The Intellectual versus the Spiritual Solution," in *The Dimensions of Job: A Study and Selected Readings*, ed. Nahum N. Glatzer (Wipf and Stock, 2002), 125.

28. Vernon J. Bourke, *Augustine's Quest for Wisdom: Life and Philosophy of the Bishop of Hippo* (Bruce, 1945), 301–2.

29. Thomas à Kempis, *The Imitation of Christ*, book 3, *On Interior Consolation*, trans. Rev. William Benham, (c. 1418–1427), chap. 15, cited in William James, *The Varieties of Religious Experience: A Study in Human Nature* (Random House Modern Library, 1902), 44.

30. Dag Hammarskjöld, *Markings*, trans. Leif Sjöberg and W. H. Auden (Vintage Books, 2006), 100.

31. *Twelve Steps and Twelve Traditions*, 99.

32. *Alcoholics Anonymous*, 63.

33. Ibid., 76.

34. Ibid., 88.

35. Bill P., Todd W., and Sara S., *Drop the Rock: Removing Character Defects: Steps Six and Seven*, 2nd ed. (Hazelden, 2005), 81.
36. William Alexander, *Ordinary Recovery: Mindfulness, Alcoholism, and the Path of Lifelong Sobriety* (Shambhala, 2010), 72–73.
37. Holy Bible: New International Version (Zondervan, 1984), 305.
38. Ibid., 307.
39. Matthew 6:9–13.
40. *Alcoholics Anonymous*, 564.
41. Ibid., 33–39.
42. Nhat Hanh, *Living Buddha*, 16.
43. Ibid., 16.
44. *Alcoholics Anonymous*, 83.
45. Ibid., 60.
46. Ibid., 568, emphasis mine.
47. *Twelve Steps and Twelve Traditions*, 106–7.
48. *Alcoholics Anonymous*, 84.
49. Ibid., 60.
50. Carl Sandberg, *Harvest Poems, 1910–1960* (Harcourt Brace Jovanovich, 1960), 38.
51. Quoted in Alfred Armand Montapert, *Distilled Wisdom* (Prentice Hall, 1973), 309.
52. James Baldwin, *The Fire Next Time* (Vintage International, 1993), 81.
53. *Alcoholics Anonymous*, 77.
54. *Dr. Bob and the Good Oldtimers: A Biography, with Recollections of Early AA in the Midwest* (Alcoholics Anonymous World Services, 1980), 338.
55. Joseph Campbell, *The Power of Myth* (Anchor Books, 1991), xiv.
56. Ibid., xiv.
57. Abraham Joshua Heschel, *I Asked for Wonder: A Spiritual Anthology*, ed. Samuel H. Dresner (Crossroad, 1983), 65.
58. *Alcoholics Anonymous*, 85.
59. Eckhart Tolle, *The Power of Now: A Guide to Spiritual Enlightenment* (New World Library, 1999), 61.

CHAPTER NINE

1. *Alcoholics Anonymous: The Story of How Many Thousands of Men and Women Recovered from Alcoholism*, 4th ed. (Alcoholics Anonymous World Services 2001), 58.

CHAPTER TEN

1. *Alcoholics Anonymous*, 83.
2. Ibid., 83.
3. Ibid., 83–84.
4. Ibid., 84.
5. Ibid., 84.
6. Ibid., 84.
7. Ibid., 84.
8. Ibid., 84.
9. Ibid., 84.
10. Ibid., 84.
11. Ibid., 60.
12. Ibid., 60.
13. Ibid., 60.

Bibliography

Alcoholics Anonymous: The Story of How Many Thousands of Men and Women Recovered from Alcoholism. 4th ed. Alcoholics Anonymous World Services, 2001.

Alexander, William. *Ordinary Recovery: Mindfulness, Alcoholism, and the Path of Lifelong Sobriety*. Shambhala, 2010.

American Psychiatric Association. *Diagnostic and Statistical Manual of Mental Disorders*. 5th ed., text rev. (DSM-5—TR). American Psychiatric Association, 2022.

American Society of Addiction Medicine. "Definition of Addiction." Updated September 15, 2019. http://www.asam.org/quality-care/definition-of-addiction.

B., Dick. *The Oxford Group and Alcoholics Anonymous: A Design for Living That Works*. Paradise Research, 1998.

Baldwin, James. *The Fire Next Time*. Vintage International, 1993.

Bourke, Vernon J. *Augustine's Quest of Wisdom: Life and Philosophy of the Bishop of Hippo*. Bruce, 1945.

Buber, Martin. *Hasidism and Modern Man*. Humanities Press International, 1958.

C., Chuck. *A New Pair of Glasses*. New-Look, 1984.

Cameron, Julia. *The Artist's Way: A Spiritual Path to Higher Creativity*. Jeremy P. Tarcher/Putnam, 1992.

Campbell, Joseph. *The Hero with a Thousand Faces*. Princeton University Press, 1949.

Campbell, Joseph. *The Power of Myth*. Anchor Books, 1991.

Carnes, Patrick. *A Gentle Path through the Twelve Steps*. Hazelden, 2012.

Covington, Stephanie S. *A Woman's Way through the Twelve Steps*. Hazelden, 1994.

Dr. Bob and the Good Oldtimers: A Biography, with Recollections of Early AA in the Midwest. Alcoholics Anonymous World Services, 1980.

Fox, Emmet. *The Sermon on the Mount: The Key to Success in Life*. Harper-SanFrancisco, 1934.

Freud, Sigmund. *On Narcissism*. 1914.

Glatzer, Nahum N., ed. *The Dimensions of Job: A Study and Selected Readings*. Wipf and Stock, 2002.

Goldberg, Rabbi Edwin, Rabbi Janet Marder, Rabbi Sheldon Marder, and Rabbi Leon Morris, eds. *Mishkan HaNefesh: Yom Kippur*. Central Conference of American Rabbis, 2015.

Hammarskjöld, Dag. *Markings*. Translated by Leif Sjöberg and W. H. Auden. Vintage Books, 2006.

Heschel, Abraham Joshua. *God in Search of Man: A Philosophy of Judaism*. Farrar, Straus, and Giroux, 1955.

Heschel, Abraham Joshua. *I Asked for Wonder: A Spiritual Anthology*. Edited by Samuel H. Dresner. Crossroad, 1983.

Hirschfield, Jerry. *The Twelve Steps for Everyone . . . Who Really Wants Them*. Hazelden, 1990.

Holy Bible: New International Version. Zondervan, 1984.

Huxley, Aldous. *The Perennial Philosophy*. Harper Perennial Modern Classics, 2009.

James, William. *The Varieties of Religious Experience: A Study in Human Nature*. Random House Modern Library, 1902.

Kabat-Zinn, Jon. *Full Catastrophe Living: Using the Wisdom of Your Body and Mind to Face Stress, Pain, and Illness*. Delacorte Press, 1990.

Kempis, Thomas à. *The Imitation of Christ*. Book 3, *On Interior Consolation*. Translated by Rev. William Benham. c. 1418–1427.

Kurtz, Ernest. *Not-God: A History of Alcoholics Anonymous*. Hazelden, 1991.

Kurtz, Ernest, and Ketcham, Katherine. *The Spirituality of Imperfection: Storytelling and the Search for Meaning*. Bantam Books, 2002.

Kushner, Harold S. *When Bad Things Happen to Good People*. Avon Books, 1981.

L., John. "Washingtonian Forebears of Alcoholics Anonymous." *AA Agnostica* (blog). July 15, 2012. https://aaagnostica.org/2012/07/15/washingtonian-forbears-of-alcoholics-anonymous/.

Marcel, Gabriel. *Homo Viator: Introduction to the Metaphysics of Hope*. St. Augustine's Press, 2010.

Mattison, Mark M., trans. "The Gospel of Thomas: A Public Domain Translation." Accessed June 13, 2023. https://www.academia.edu/15107954/The_Gospel_of_Thomas_A_Public_Domain_Translation.

Montapert, Alfred Armand. *Distilled Wisdom*. Prentice Hall, 1973.

Mowrer, O. Hobart. "Small Groups in Historical Perspective." In *Explorations in Self-Help and Mutual Aid*, edited by Leonard D. Borman. Center for Urban Studies, Northwestern University, 1974.

Murphy, Michael. *Golf in the Kingdom*. Penguin Random House, 2022.

Nhat Hanh, Thich. *Living Buddha, Living Christ*. Riverhead Books, 1995.

Nemeck, Francis K., and Marie T. Coombs, *O Blessed Night! Recovering from Addiction, Codependency, and Attachment Based on the Insights of St. John of the Cross and Pierre Teilhard de Chardin*. Alba House, 1991.

P., Bill, Todd W., and Sara S. *Drop the Rock: Removing Character Defects: Steps Six and Seven*. 2nd ed. Hazelden, 2005.

"Pass It On": Bill Wilson and How the AA Message Reached the World (Alcoholics Anonymous, 1984), 368

Pittman, Bill. *Stepping Stones to Recovery*. Glen Abbey Books, 1988.

Sandburg, Carl. *Harvest Poems, 1910–1960*. Harcourt Brace Jovanovich, 1960.

Schaberg, William H. *Writing "The Big Book": The Creation of AA*. Central Recovery Press, 2019.

Shoemaker, Helen Smith. *I Stand by the Door: The Life of Sam Shoemaker*. Word Books, 1967.

Stein, Murray. *Jung's Map of the Soul*. Open Court, 1998.

Steinberg, Milton. *Basic Judaism*. Harcourt Brace, 1947.

Thomsen, Robert. *Bill W.* Harper and Row, 1975.

Thurman, Howard. *Meditations of the Heart*. Beacon Press, 1981.

Tillich, Paul. *The Courage to Be*. Yale University Press, 1952.

"Time 100 Persons of the Century." *Time*, June 14, 1999. https://content.time .com/time/magazine/article/0,9171,26473,00.html.

Tolle, Eckhart. *The Power of Now: A Guide to Spiritual Enlightenment*. New World Library, 1999.

Twelve Steps and Twelve Traditions. Alcoholics Anonymous, 1953.

Twerski, Abraham J. *The Spiritual Self: Reflections on Recovery and God*. Hazelden, 2000.

W., Bill. *Alcoholics Anonymous Comes of Age: A Brief History of AA*. Alcoholics Anonymous, 1957.

———. *The Language of the Heart: Bill W.'s Grapevine Writings*. AA Grapevine, 1988.

White, William L. *Slaying the Dragon: The History of Addiction Treatment and Recovery in America*. Chestnut Health Systems/Lighthouse Institute, 2014.

Suggested Reading

Any or all the books listed in the bibliography (although some more than others) are worthwhile reading material for someone who has a desire to explore further the topics of recovery, the twelve steps, Alcoholics Anonymous, the heroic journey, or spirituality. Listed here are excellent books that aren't quoted in this book. This is far from a complete survey of excellent books on these subjects, but they represent a good beginning. Some authors included in the bibliography have written other excellent books worthy of your time, including but not limited to Abraham Joshua Heschel, Thomas Merton, and Thich Nhat Hanh. I hope your reading experience is as enjoyable and edifying for you as mine has been for me.

B., Mel. *My Search for Bill W.* Hazelden, 2000.
———. *New Wine: The Spiritual Roots of the Twelve Step Miracle.* Hazelden, 1991.
Brand, Russell. *Recovery: Freedom from Our Addictions.* Bluebird, 2017.
Campbell, Joseph. *The Hero with a Thousand Faces.* 2nd ed. Princeton University Press, 1968.
F., Andy. *The Twelve Steps for Agnostics.* Independently published, April 2018.
Griffin, Kevin, *One Breath at a Time: Buddhism and the Twelve Steps.* Rodale, 2017.
Grisel, Judith, *Never Enough: The Neuroscience and Experience of Addiction.* Doubleday, 2019.
Harbaugh, Jim. *A 12-Step Approach to the Spiritual Exercises of St. Ignatius.* Sheed and Ward, 1997.

Hayman, Ronald. *A Life of Jung*. W. W. Norton, 1999.

Jung, Carl. *The Portable Jung*. Translated by R. F. C. Hull. Viking Press, 1971.

Lamott, Anne. *Plan B: Further Thoughts on Faith*. Riverhead Books, 2005.

Lattin, Don. *Distilled Spirits: Getting High, Then Sober, with a Famous Writer, a Forgotten Philosopher, and a Hopeless Drunk*. University of California Press, 2012.

Leeming, David. *Myth: A Biography of Belief*. Oxford University Press, 2002.

McCabe, Ian. *Carl Jung and Alcoholics Anonymous: The Twelve Steps as a Spiritual Journey of Individuation*. Routledge, 2018.

Merton, Thomas. *No Man Is an Island*. Harcourt Brace Jovanovich, 1955.

Olitzky, Rabbi Kerry M., and Stuart A. Copans. *Twelve Jewish Steps to Recovery: A Personal Guide to Turning from Alcoholism and Other Addictions*. 2nd ed. Jewish Lights, 2009.

Osbon, Diane K. *A Joseph Campbell Compendium: Reflections on the Art of Living*. Harper Perennial, 1991.

Pearson, Carol S. *Awakening the Heroes Within: Twelve Archetypes to Help Us Find Ourselves and Transform the World*. HarperSanFrancisco, 1991.

Rohr, Richard. *Breathing under Water: Spirituality and the Twelve Steps*. 2nd ed. Franciscan Media, 2021.

S., Laura. *12 Steps on Buddha's Path: Bill, Buddha, and We: A Spiritual Journal of Recovery*. Wisdom, 2006.

Schoen, David E. *The War of the Gods in Addiction: C. G. Jung, Alcoholics Anonymous, and Archetypal Evil*. Spring Journal Books, 2009.

Segal, Robert A. *Joseph Campbell: An Introduction*. Rev. ed. Penguin Books, 1990.

Steinberg, Rabbi Paul. *Recovery, the 12 Steps, and Jewish Spirituality: Reclaiming Hope, Courage, and Wholeness*. Jewish Lights, 2014.

Storr, Anthony. *The Essential Jung*. Princeton University Press, 1983.

Taub, Rabbi Shais. *God of Our Understanding: Jewish Spirituality and Recovery from Addiction*. KATV, 2011.

Index